Good Dad, Bad Dad: A Journey Through Parenting Choices

Exploring the Fine Line Between Nurture and Harshness

by Oluremi Makinde

INDEX

Hey there, Awesome Reader!

Welcome to an adventure that's bound to change everything you thought you knew! This book, packed with insights, explorations, and revelations, was born from a swirling storm of ideas, sleepless nights, and more coffee than I care to admit. Let's face it—you're here because something caught your interest, and I promise you, it's going to be one hell of a ride.

The purpose of this book is crystal clear: to dive headfirst into the themes that matter most—life, love, struggle, and triumph. It wasn't always easy, you know? There were plenty of moments when I thought about tossing my laptop out the window and calling it a day. But through the ups and the downs, I remained determined to unravel the threads of my thoughts and weave them into a tapestry that I hope resonates with you.

Throughout the writing process, I delved deep into research, exploring various perspectives, unearthing hidden gems of knowledge, and wrestling with my own experiences. Each chapter has been carefully crafted, infused with passion and a raw desire to connect with you on a profound level. I wracked my brain, asked for feedback, and restructured sentences more times than I can count to ensure that it flows like a river, inviting you to dive in.

What you'll find within these pages isn't just an ordinary read; it's a conversation, a connection, and an exploration. Consider it a window into my mind and a mirror reflecting our collective experiences. I invite you to challenge ideas, embrace new perspectives, and perhaps even laugh out loud at the absurdity of it all. Trust me, there's a little bit of everything tucked away here.

As you embark on this journey, I encourage you to keep your heart and mind wide open. Each word has a purpose—to spark something within you, to encourage thought, to inspire action. We live in a time where stories matter more than ever, and I'm thrilled to share mine with you. This is not just about me; it's about us and the shared human experience.

Throughout these chapters, you'll come across stories that touch on the highs and lows of life, the beauty found in struggle, and the joy in discovery. I hope you can relate, resonate, and, dare I say, even find solace in the pages that follow. When you reach the end, my greatest hope is that you'll walk away feeling empowered and perhaps a little changed.

So, buckle up! You're not just flipping through a book; you're delving into a world where every sentence pulls you further into the intrigue and excitement of human existence. This is your invitation to lose yourself in the rhythm of my words and emerge with new thoughts swirling in your mind.

I can't wait for you to experience each chapter, to feel the emotions, to laugh, cry, and contemplate along the way. Together, let's venture into the unknown, explore the depths of our souls, and expose the raw truths of life that bind us all.

Thank you for being here, for opting into this journey with me. Your presence is invaluable, and I am beyond excited to share what I've created. It's time to let the adventure unfold. Let's go!

Here's to discovery, connection, and the beautiful chaos that is life. You ready? I sure am!

With all my enthusiasm and energy!

The Shadow and the Light

Alex's Crossroads

Alex stood by the window, his hands resting on the cool surface of the glass, watching his son outside. It was a warm afternoon, sunshine filtering through tree branches and casting dappled patterns on the grass. Little Ethan was on the swing, legs pumping like a little engine, laughter spilling into the air like music. Each swing felt like a moment in eternity, a pure slice of childhood joy.

But while the sounds of laughter reverberated through the stillness of the afternoon, Alex's mind was a whirlpool of thoughts, dragging him underwater into the depths of his own past. His heart felt heavy with the weight of choice, with the looming uncertainty of his newfound role as a father. In that serene moment, enveloped by the laughter of his son and the vibrant colors of the world outside, Alex felt the painful clash of contrasting memories.

He closed his eyes for a brief moment, allowing the memories to wash over him. They unfurled like a meticulously woven tapestry, rich in warmth and textured with complexities. There he was again, a small boy of seven, enveloped in his father's embrace after a long day of school. His dad had a way of wrapping his arms around him that made the troubles of the world fade away. Alex could almost feel the strength and safety of that hug; the smell of his father's aftershave mingling with the scent of grass from their backyard.

“Everything will be okay, buddy. Just believe in yourself,” his father had whispered, tucking him into bed. Those soft words echoed fondly in Alex’s mind, offering a sanctuary against the anxieties of the world. Warm hugs, bedtime stories filled with adventure, and the tender encouragement that followed him through childhood replayed like a beloved movie. His father instilled confidence in him, allowing him to dream, to reach for the stars without the fear of falling short.

Yet, intertwined with those memories were the stark images of his best friend, Jake, raised under a different banner. Jake's father was an emblem of strict discipline, silent yet demanding in his expectations. He remembered viscerally the moments where laughter was cut short, replaced by sharp criticisms during swim practice, where success was measured not in joy but in relentless standards. The juxtaposition was jarring—a world where love was accompanied by stern lectures, where hugs were few and hard-earned.

A vivid memory struck Alex next, one of a practice that had pushed Jake to his emotional limits, culminating in a night that remained scarred in his memory. Jake had come to Alex's house later that evening, his shoulders drooping, his face pale. The humiliation of disappointing his father had choked him like a weighted blanket, wrapping him in fear and despair. Alex had offered his friend a snack and a distraction, wishing he could shoulder some of that pain, but they both knew it would linger.

He opened his eyes again and looked outside, noticing how Ethan had now moved on to building a castle in the sandbox, each scoop of sand sent flying in his concentrated effort. There was a sweet innocence in his son's determination, a raw purity that Alex marveled at.

"Who will you be?" he whispered, internally questioning what kind of father he wanted to be. Would he choose the security of nurturing love or the rigorous expectations of discipline? The childhood decisions his own parents made were etched in the fibers of his being, and the shadows of their choices haunted him. Alex bit his lip, torn between the echoes of encouragement from his own father and the stringent lessons his friend had endured.

He recalled how often he had daydreamed about being a father, envisioning a blend of both those worlds; perhaps with the nurturing he cherished but bolstered by the resolve he admired from Jake's father. Was it possible to provide gentle guidance while instilling the discipline that crafted resilience?

The fear of repeating history gnawed at him like an uninvited guest, whispering doubts that coursed through his mind. What if he became too lenient? Or worse, what if he became too hard? Would Ethan grow to resent him or seek solace in someone else's stern embrace? Memories danced with uncertainty, each step Alex took along this precarious path felt like a tightrope walk stretching high over an endless chasm.

"Will I succeed?" he murmured to himself, searching the depths of his fears. His father had always encouraged him to reach for the stars, but he now faced a new kind of pressure—the pressure of shaping a new life, of teaching his son the essential lessons of the world without losing sight of their connection.

Watching Ethan play, the innocent joy radiating in his laughter, Alex allowed the memory to unfurl deeper, challenging him with scenes from his upbringing. There was the time they went fishing—a simple outing, yet pivotal. His father had curated that day, gently teaching Alex the patience required in casting lines and the joys of simple successes like reeling in the tiniest of fish. It was not just about fishing; it was about savoring the quiet moments and learning that patience often bore the greatest fruits.

But juxtaposing that was the recollection of a moment at the pool where Jake's father had shouted at him for misjudging a dive, shaking the boy and demanding he never made that mistake again. Alex had cringed as he watched his friend flounder through the water, his eyes welling with unshed tears yet refusing to cry. Jake was praised for success but scarred by the expectations attached.

As he looked back out the window, lost in memories of his childhood, Alex found himself questioning his approach. He wanted to offer his son the same reassurance his father had bestowed upon him—the reassurance that mistakes were part of growing, that the power of choosing kindness and compassion shaped the heart. Yet at the same time, he understood there needed to be boundaries, a structure that could guide Ethan without overshadowing his spirit.

The memories swirled in the confines of his brain—each one wrestling with another—creating a cacophony of ideals. The gentle embrace of his father mixed with the sharp tone of Jake's dad; one taught compassion, the other instilled fear of failure. The mixture was intoxicating and immobilizing. Which path would he choose for Ethan?

"Alex, come on!" Ethan's voice broke into his thoughts, a beacon of youthful exuberance, drawing him back into the moment.

Alex smiled, feeling the warmth of his son's energy pierce through the fog of confusion. "I'm right here, buddy!" He finally stepped away from the window, the weight of decision refusing to be hidden, but softened by the simple truth of how much he loved his son.

He joined Ethan outside, kneeling beside him in the shimmering sunlight. The sand slipped through his fingers, a pragmatism accompanying the innocence of youth. A castle awaited construction, a world connected through pieces of sand, laughter, and time.

And as he watched Ethan scoop and pile sand, Alex came to a realization—parenting was not meant to be a dichotomy but a dance, one that embraced both nurturing and discipline fluidly. It was about guiding while offering freedom, teaching without stifling, and providing love interwoven with strength.

In this heartfelt reflection, Alex felt a glimmer of hope, a foundation upon which he could build. This was not just a journey of comparison, of warring ideals; it was about choosing to forge a path uniquely his own, enriched by the lessons learned from his father's warm guiding light and the stern shadows that accompanied his best friend's upbringing.

"Let's build the biggest castle, Daddy!" Ethan enthused, pulling Alex from his thoughts.

"Absolutely! But remember," Alex said, guiding a handful of sand, "we need a solid foundation, just like how we were talking about making our dreams come true. It takes teamwork."

The expression on Ethan's face transformed into one of earnest concentration, and for a moment, it felt like a pact formed; a shared understanding that while every father may walk a different path, they both carried an innate desire to succeed in this journey of growth. In that moment, Alex resolved that he would strive to become the father that blended nurturing with the strength learned from the lessons of their lives—never shying away from the shadows of doubt, always reaching toward the light.

The Influence of Two Fathers

Alex stood in the kitchen, the aroma of breakfast filling the air, his mind lingering somewhere far away from the warm glow of the morning sun streaming through the window. As he whipped up scrambled eggs, he couldn't shake off the weight of two contrasting parental legacies that loomed in his thoughts. His father, warm and nurturing, represented everything tender. He remembered the way his father would gather him into a cozy bear hug, wrapping him in security, quelling fears of a world that could be harsh and unkind.

In stark contrast stood the figure of his best friend's father, a man shaped by the rigid lines of discipline. The stern lines of his features, the powerful voice that commanded respect, felt like a fortress built on the foundation of 'tough love.' While he deep down admired the strength and success his friend had garnered through years of strict upbringing, Alex often felt the subtle echo of sacrifice woven into every triumphant tale. As the eggs began to congeal in the pan, his mind wandered back to moments when these two influences shaped his understanding of fatherhood.

His father's influence was like a gentle river, meandering peacefully, nourishing the banks with love and patience. He recalled how on rainy afternoons, they would curl up on the couch, his father reading stories replete with dreams of adventure. The warmth of those moments filled the air with idealism, and Alex learned a visceral appreciation for emotional connection. "It's okay to feel, son," his father would say, his voice soft and reassuring. "Your dreams are worth holding onto, and it's perfectly fine to share them." Not once did his father belittle his feelings or experiences, instead weaving them into lessons that taught resilience through gentle encouragement.

Yet, standing in the shadows of his best friend's upbringing, Alex couldn't help but also admire the unyielded determination of discipline shown by Mr. Harris. Alex remembered his friend Ryan recounting tales of early morning practices and hard-earned victories won through sweat and strict instruction.

"I don't care if you don't like it; it's good for you," Mr. Harris would bark, his voice echoing in their universe like an immutable law. While Ryan thrived under the pressure, guilt weighed on Alex. When they met for lunch, his heart swelled at the success glinting in Ryan's eyes, yet it was invariably paired with an unnerving cloud that shadowed Alex's perception of the cost behind that success. The camaraderie they shared was tinged with an unspoken understanding of the emotional hurdles that came with that victorious pursuit.

What Alex witnessed in Ryan was a struggle laced with pride, an accomplishment tinged with anxiety. As he continued flipping the eggs in the pan, he felt frustration bubble within him. He admired his father for the confidence he instilled, while his admiration for Mr. Harris remained tinged with skepticism. Was discipline the true path to success, or was there a possibility that warmth and connection were equally powerful? The steady fluctuations between admiration and skepticism left him trapped in a vortex of conflicting ideals.

Made even more complex by societal expectations—Alex grappled with the notion of what a father 'should' be. Society seemed to hold an unyielding decree that fathers must be strong, a little rough around the edges, echoing the praises of relentless determination. Culture often painted a picture of success achieved through an iron-fisted approach, but it also spoke of emotional availability as merely secondary. He carried that dissonance like a burden,

"Be tough, yet vulnerable," a voice in society would chime. "Show love through strength, but never lose sight of who you are." The contradictions should beckon clarity, but instead, they only echoed confusion, exacerbating the internal conflict Alex faced—how could he pull from two fathers, two powerful yet divergent ideals at once?

In his father, Alex saw vision, a man who cherished creativity while passing it on. "Life is too grand to be lived without dreams," his father often proclaimed, guiding Alex to envision worlds beyond what was. Yet as Alex stood on the fringes of becoming a father himself, he found himself straddling that fine line between nurturing and discipline, caught between the familiar warmth of encouragement and the relentless pursuit of discipline exemplified through Mr. Harris's harshness.

Instinctively, Alex longed for the safety that accompanied softness but felt the weighty hand of expectations urging him toward fortitude. He questioned what kind of father he could be as images of both his father and Mr. Harris floated in his mind like specters haunting his resolve. He pictured himself as a father in the moment—tenderly encouraging yet equally assertive, just as he observed in Mr. Harris's son's success.

Despite the comfort provided by his father's love, there was always an underlying mistrust of safety; a discomfort in simply allowing love to flourish without the hard edge of expectation. The contrasting teachings painted a fragmented picture in Alex's mind—who was he to dismiss the accomplishments rooted in discipline?

Breakfast assembled, Alex finally sat at the small table, his son happily munching on toast, giggling about something whimsical. He found himself caught, even at this moment, gazing at his own child with longing. He wanted so desperately to embody the warmth he had known yet still feared failure lingered alongside ideals cultivated in strictness.

As he observed his son's uneventful curiosity, his imagination ignited with wonder, a glimmer of innocence shining through the mundanity. He craved to nurture that spirit and prime him for the world ahead. Yet, could he ignore the lessons learned from Ryan? The value of discipline had its merits. There were elements of strength hidden within firmness, and Alex wished to extract those lessons without straying from compassion.

The day moved on in a blur of chaotic remarks from peers at the park, where the intricacies of fatherhood rippled beneath the surface like treacherous undercurrents. Alex saw fathers chuckle with their children, steamrolling the seriousness of adulthood through laughter, grounding their little ones in the reality of wholesome allowance. In those moments, he felt a soft tug inside, yearning to be among them, to laugh freely with his son, yet sometimes watching from the sidelines left him lost.

He felt stunted in action as fleeting shadowy comparisons whispered echoes of both ideological extremes. The children waddled with joy, lost in blameless, carefree play. Parents chattered, some dishing out correction while others resorted to gentle nudges towards safety—each their own balance of discipline mixed with encouragement. As Alex intervened between the children's quarrels, guiding his son toward a kinder resolution, he could feel the pressures beginning to weigh on him.

Would he be the father who would kneel to listen and slowly dispel doubt, or would he be harsh? Every interaction brought another reminder of how significant that balance was amidst his mental tug of war.

The confusion gnawed at him—what should he be emulating? He could see the glows of encouragement illuminated in his father's approach, while beside him stood the relentless discipline embodied by Mr. Harris. It was as though they were two mountains nestled along either side of Alex, their looming shadows enveloping him with heavy considerations.

In moments of clarity, Alex began to accept the validity of each approach to fatherhood. The tenderness distilling from his dad should carve his unwritten style, yet there was value cradled in the stoic determination his friend's father so often dispensed. He was beginning to understand that it wasn't merely about choosing one path over the other; rather, it was about weaving them together into a unique tapestry.

The blending of ideals felt simultaneously invigorating and overwhelming. Alex's aspirations took shape as he better navigated the ground he stood on, filled with thoughts of what kind of father he would become. As uncertainty lingered, he could lean into warmer embraces while preserving the lessons instilled through discipline. It was about seeking that harmony within the scattered ideals that filled his mind.

That notion of balance was transformative. Looking back, he knew he needed to grasp from both worlds—mingle that warmth with discipline's urgency while desperately leaning into the understanding that vulnerability wasn't weakness, but strength when appropriately applied. The external pressures needn't shackle him; he simply had to redefine the expectations through the lens of love and be willing to combine those realities with intention.

As he held his son's hand, Alex reveled in the simple joy, the extraordinary thrill derived from their whimsical interactions. He knew there would be moments of conflict, incomplete ideas, and layered mistakes ahead. Still, he felt a comforting pulse of determination that coursed through him—the assurance that navigating faithfully between conflicting ideals was precisely where he needed to stand.

To honor both sides was to honor himself, as he wove together the legacies of two fathers within himself—infusing both warmth and strength into a fatherhood uniquely his own.

The Birth of Doubt

As the sun dipped below the horizon, casting a warm glow across the living room, Alex stood at the window, his hands resting against the cool glass, watching his son play in the backyard. The scene was idyllic. His son, Caleb, was chasing the last rays of sunlight, his laughter echoing against the muted backdrop of the evening. For a fleeting moment, the beauty of the scene overwhelmed Alex, filling him with a profound sense of pride. But just as quickly, a shroud of doubt cloaked his heart, darkening the edges of the joy that flared within him.

Alex's mind drifted back to his own childhood, where echoes of laughter and the warmth of familial love mingled with the sharp shadow of fear that loomed over him. Memories flickered like a film reel, images fragmented yet vivid, encapsulating the moments that defined him. He could almost feel the tender touch of his father's hand on his shoulder, hear the words of encouragement being spoken softly after every triumphant or failed attempt. But eclipsing it all was the gnawing worry that he would one day disappoint that same figure, just as he feared he might fail his own son.

As the wind rustled the leaves of the nearby trees, intertwining joy and anxiety, Alex felt a frisson of doubt slither through him. His own childhood was painted in gentle hues of security—stories woven as bedtime rituals and daily hugs filled with understanding. Yet clawing through it all was the gnawing fear that he was standing at a precipice, unsure of which path to take as a father. Would he be nurturing like his own dad? Or would he become the type of strict disciplinarian that his best friend's father had been?

His thoughts turned chaotic, a torrential downpour in the intimate corners of his mind. Memories of his father's gentle guidance clashed violently with the images of his friend's father, a figure carved from stone, whose relentless drive for discipline loomed large. The warm brown eyes of his father contrasted sharply against the piercing cold glare that his friend received. Time and again, he witnessed both men shape young lives through their varying philosophies. Each man taught valuable lessons, but in their footsteps lay the roots of a confusing legacy.

Would he nurture and foster his son's dreams, or would he push Caleb toward performance, focusing solely on success? It was a tightrope walk, uncertainty churning beneath his feet. As he watched Caleb tumble lightly in the grass, the cool breeze intermingling with the fragrant scent of blooming flowers, Alex felt the weight of impending decisions settle heavily on his chest. His heart raced, echoing the rhythm of his tangled thoughts—how could he balance love and discipline without falling into the pitfalls that had marked his upbringing?

The sunlight began to fade, bathing the yard in shadows, and Alex's heart sank with it. Trees that once stood tall and vibrant morphed into menacing silhouettes. His childhood memories erupted like volcanoes within him—raw, emotional landscapes where the borders of love were often blurred. He could hear the ever-looming disappointment in his father's voice during moments of perceived failure. His dad, though always supportive, had moments of sharp critique when things did not go as envisioned, seeping through the words that were meant to heal. The emotional scars attached to those moments flickered in his thoughts, filling him with a profound sense of dread.

Alex pressed a hand to his heart, feeling it race as if desperately trying to shield him from this onslaught of uncomfortable history. Those shadows etched fear into his mind: fear of inadequate parenting, fear of repeating history, fear of ultimately becoming that which he despised. It was an unforgiving cycle that wrapped around him like vines, squeezing tighter with every step forward.

Caleb's laughter filtered through the air again, piercing the oppressive fog of anxiety that would not relent, but the sounds were muffled, an echo of joy tainted by the clashing doubts that surfed the waves of Alex's consciousness. "What if you're not good enough for him?" a voice whispered from within. "What if your choices lead him down a path of discontent?" The wild storm of questioning buried deeper into him, a tempest raging uncontrollably.

He recalled moments when he faltered, when he felt he hadn't met the expectations he placed on himself—the time he lost patience during a hectic evening or snapped at Caleb for a small mess made during playtime. The weight of those lapses now pressed against him like a cloud of shadows, suffocating the sun's warm glow. In the recesses of his mind, the nebulous specter of disappointment, the realization that he might recreate this chasm between father and son, festered and fumed.

As Alex gazed out at the sprawl of his backyard, he couldn't help but see it through the lens of turmoil. Each blade of grass, every laugh exchanged in this serene moment became tainted by the haunting thoughts of past errors, lost opportunities, and the relentless ticking of the clock that reminded him that every moment mattered. How he longed to capture it all in a state of perfection—a perfect fatherhood. Yet, lurking beneath that desire was an equally formidable fear: the notion of imperfection lurking just around the corner, waiting to pounce.

Time stretched and twisted, warping his sense of reality. Images morphed in his mind, creating a plethora of absurd scenarios: what if he pushed too hard? What if he was not strict enough? What if Caleb later resented him for not having discipline in his life? Those thoughts dove inside of him, swirling violently, and clouding the warmth of his father's embrace in his memories.

How could he be anything but a reflection of the two contrasting fathers? The warrior nurturing versus the ironfisted guardian. Each figure loomed larger than life in his psyche, casting their long shadows upon his aspirations and fears. Every time he turned a corner, reaching for clarity, he found himself plunging deeper into confusion instead—a dark abyss curling around his thoughts, pulling him further into its depths.

And in the depths, Alex found himself on the verge of tears—frustration bubbling like a spring ready to erupt. He struck out against the turmoil within. "Why can't it be simple? Why can't I just be the father I want to be?" With each suppressed sob, each suppressed scream, he felt he wasn't just fighting to be good enough for Caleb, but good enough for the almighty legacy of fatherhood.

It was in this swirling chaos that Alex began to confront the core of his doubt—the fear of being judged not just by his son, but by himself. His own expectations became a noose, tightening around his neck, squeezing out rational thought and filling the void with distress. Standing poised at the threshold of fatherhood, he finally recognized that the most intimidating aspect wasn't just parenting itself, but the looming figure of his own self-doubt.

He shook his head, trying to clear the tumult within, seeking reprieve in mundane realities. The laughter of his son echoed around him, blending with the tangible warmth of daylight almost extinguished. With every rise and fall of his son's small frame, Alex fought against the tide of uncertainty that rose to drown him. It was within that connection, that visceral bond between father and son, that he might yet unearth the strength to rise above the maelstrom brewing inside.

Alex stepped back from the window, retreating from the encroaching shadows, refusing to succumb further to those feelings of inadequacy. For now, he could choose to step outside, to find perspective in reality rather than allowing the tremors of his fears to claw at him. As he opened the door and stepped onto the porch, he inhaled deeply, filling his lungs with the fragrance of fresh-cut grass, mingled with the earthy notes of soil.

"Caleb!" he called out, attempting to infuse his voice with buoyancy. His son turned, his small face breaking into a wide grin that instantly warmed Alex's heart. In that moment, the memory of his own father's embrace echoed again, yet this time without the distorting lens of doubt, allowing for clarity in the joy of connection.

As the two bound toward one another, Alex felt the shadows of fear dissipating slightly, like a cloud shifting to reveal the sun hidden behind. This interaction promised a flicker of hope, a chance—a shared adventure between father and son that held limitless potential. Each laugh, each embrace could reshape the dark thoughts that had begun to define his narrative.

The wild thoughts that had filled his mind just moments ago now felt less daunting, fading like wisps of fog once illuminated by the sun breaking through at dawn. While Alex was far from eradicating every shadow that threatened his confidence, he realized, perhaps for the first time, that it was within the uncertainties and the imperfections that lay the essential lessons for his journey ahead.

Alex reflected on his father, and the very teachings, amidst imperfections, were what truly built bridges of understanding. With each step forward, he could redefine what it meant to nurture, to blend the lessons of love with that of discipline, and ultimately create an environment for Caleb to thrive.

And as they played under the fading light, racing against the approaching night, Alex began to realize that his journey would be fraught with doubt but was also filled with tremendous promise, a chance not just to guide his son but to grow alongside him.

In the end, it was not about eliminating the fears that echoed within him—it was about learning to carry them, acknowledging their presence while maintaining the resolve to move forward. It was at that moment, encased in laughter and the warmth of familial love, that he committed himself to being a father who dared to embrace both the sunshine and the shadows that accompanied the journey of parenting.

Echoes of My Childhood

A Gentle Embrace

The late afternoon sun filtered through the oak tree in the backyard, casting a warm glow into the family home. Sounds of laughter echoed from outside as Alex chased after his friends, their gleeful shouts bubbling over with joy and innocence, but not all was well within him. That day, the weight of the world rested heavily on his tiny shoulders. It wasn't something he could articulate—not at his age—yet the feeling lingered: a gnawing discomfort that made his heart race with uncertainty.

As he stomped inside, the door creaked softly, groaning from years of memories. The familiar scent of apple pie baking in the oven lingered in the air—a comforting aroma that had the power to soothe and heal. He could hear his father's voice humming a tune, a gentle, rhythmic melody that had woven its way into the very fabric of his childhood. But as he caught sight of his father in the kitchen, a swirl of emotions crashed over him. His dad stood at the counter, a cheerful figure caught in the ballet of daily life, kneading dough with deft hands, flour dusting his cheeks like confetti celebrating an unremarkable day.

“Hey, buddy! You want to help me with these pastries?” his father called out, a hint of mischief dancing in his tone. The smile that spread across his face was welcoming and warm, radiant like the sun shining through the window behind him—yet today, Alex felt far from jubilant.

“No,” he muttered, his voice barely above a whisper as he slumped into one of the kitchen chairs, his head resting on the cool oak table. He was exhausted, both physically and emotionally, and the enormity of it all crept steadily into view. The laughter from outside faded away, replaced by an internal storm of confusion and doubt that raged within him.

His father tilted his head, concern etched on his brow as he watched Alex’s posture—defeated and small. “What’s wrong, Alex?” Without waiting for a response, he stepped away from the counter, wiping his hands on a damp cloth, and approached his son, whose world seemed to have narrowed down to a single heavy heart.

The short walk from the counter seemed to carry both weight and grace. In that moment, Alex could see the love pooling in his father's eyes, an unwavering depth that promised solace. His dad knelt beside him, enveloping him in the familiar scent of his cologne mixed with the dough in the air, and slowly wrapped his arms around him. A gentle embrace.

In that instant, the storm within Alex quieted, and he melted into the solidity of his father's grasp, feeling safe and protected within those strong arms. The warmth enveloped him like a cozy blanket on a cold winter night, washing over him and reminding him that it was okay to feel. “It’s alright to have bad days, you know,” his father whispered softly, as he smoothed Alex’s hair back with a tender touch. “I’m here for you.”

The embrace was not just a physical connection; it was an unspoken understanding that Alex had come to cherish throughout his childhood. It was more than the act of holding him; it was a waiting kind of love, a space created for Alex to unleash whatever burdens he carried inside. In the cocoon of that hug, the worries that crowded his mind began to slip away, like strands of fog dispersing in the morning light.

It was funny, he thought. He couldn’t quite remember a specific event that had triggered the sadness, but the weight sat comfortably on his shoulders—a concoction of stress from school, the anxiety of fitting in with the other children, worries about whether or not he would be liked. All those swirling thoughts ebbed softly in the space of his father’s embrace.

“Do you want to talk about it?” his father asked gently, not pressuring him but inviting him toward sharing his heart. There was no rush, no urgency, just that calm, steady presence that had always allowed Alex to feel seen and heard.

After a moment, the words slid out of his mouth like a timid whisper. “I just... I don’t know. I feel like everyone expects me to be perfect.”

His father nodded, his grip tightening a fraction, as though trying to infuse Alex with a little more strength of his own. “I know it can feel that way sometimes. But perfection isn’t real, son. It’s okay to make mistakes. Do you know what my dad used to tell me?”

Alex looked up, curiosity piercing through the haze of his worries. "What?"

"Life is about learning. Sometimes you win, and sometimes you lose. But as long as you keep trying, that's what counts."

There was something in his father's tone, a woven texture of experience mixed with love. It was an echo of strength that resonated deeply within Alex, a soothing balm attending to exposed wounds he did not even know he bore.

"I just want to be liked," he mumbled, uncertainty lingering in his voice.

His father pulled back slightly, enough to meet Alex's gaze. "You are already liked, buddy. You have friends who care about you. Remember, they like you for who you are, not for what you accomplish."

As Alex absorbed those words, he felt the warmth of his father's embrace wrapping him tightly once more, a gentle cocoon against the harshness of the outside world. Each repetition of the hug created a fortress around his heart where vulnerability was welcomed and understood—a safe harbor amidst the tempest of expectations.

"How about we make some cookies together?" his father suggested, a tease igniting a spark of joy in the melancholy air. "I'll show you my secret ingredient."

A smile broke through the clouds of Alex's discomfort, lifting his spirit like a kite catching the wind. "What is it?"

"Love," his father declared proudly, and they both shared a laughter that rang out joyously, a melody of connection that seemed to stitch together the raw edges of the day. Even the scuff of tiredness retreated into the corners of the room.

In that moment of ease, the world outside no longer seemed daunting. They rose together, side by side, as they began to gather ingredients—flour pouring like soft snowfall onto the counter, eggs cracked open revealing their gold, and sugar sparkled in the sunlight like tiny diamonds against the wood. Each step of the process became a dance they shared, fostering an atmosphere rich with laughter, sweet remnants of hope, and the promise of understanding.

They became absorbed in transforming raw ingredients into something beautiful, much like the transformation that Alexander felt happening within himself. The skills learned in the kitchen—patience, excitement, attention to detail, even the occasional mess—would steep him not only in the flavor of pastries but in the essence of life itself. Baking became more than an activity; it was a gentle reminder of the beauty found in companionship, in nurturing, and in the love generously shared in the simple gifts of life.

As they pulled the cookies out of the oven, a wave of warmth flooded the kitchen, enveloping them both again—a different kind of embrace filled with the promise of sweetness. Alex could hardly contain his excitement, his earlier worries washed away, and a radiant smile illuminated his face. This glorious moment burned brightly in his memory and became a touchstone he would carry with him through the years.

That memory stayed etched in Alex's heart, a gentle reminder of the nurturing love his father provided. Throughout his life, he would encounter challenges filled with uncertainty and pressures that threatened to pull him under. But during those moments, he would picture that warm embrace—the feeling of being enveloped in love, both strong and gentle, teaching him the vital lesson that it was okay to feel vulnerable, that gentleness could be a fortifying strength.

Years later, as Alex became a father himself, he often revisited that moment in the kitchen. He understood then that it wasn't just a memory—it was a foundation. It was the embodiment of patience and understanding that his father had imparted so generously, a legacy of love that would guide him through the labyrinth of fatherhood.

Alex hoped to uphold and nurture that same spirit in his relationship with his son, to hold him close in moments of joy as well as in times of distress. Just as his father had taught him the warmth contained within those small yet profound gestures of gentleness, Alex yearned to weave that same quality into the fabric of his own parenting style.

He envisioned moments filled with laughter in the kitchen—sugar flying in the air during baking escapades, their playful banter echoing similar sentiments of love shared by his own father. In those moments, they would create a safe harbor, allowing his son to express his emotions, to stumble and fall, and to find delight amid the chaos just as he had.

The gentle embrace of nurturing would guide their adventures, allowing tenderness to become intertwined with discipline, so each choice could resonate with compassion and understanding. With every step forward, Alex carried the echoes of his childhood, ready to breed them anew within the heart of his young family.

Whether in happiness or sorrow, it was in these gentle embraces that Alex found solace—a treasure trove of warmth spreading roots deep into his soul, guiding him every day as he navigated the beautiful, difficult, and ever-evolving journey of fatherhood.

Lessons on Patience

As Alex sat on the porch, the sunlight danced through the leaves of the maple tree in their front yard, creating playful shadows that flickered across the grass. He could see his son, Jamie, chasing after a butterfly, laughter ringing out like a melody through the crisp air. The innocence of childhood enveloped them both, but it also sparked a wave of nostalgia in Alex, making him reflect on the lessons he learned from his own father—lessons that emphasized connection over performance and the extraordinary power of patience.

He recalled the days spent with his dad by the serene surface of Lake Whitley, where he learned that fishing was not merely about catching the biggest trout but about tranquility and time shared together. Those weekend mornings were sacred. They would rise before dawn, the world still wrapped in a veil of sleep as they quietly prepared their gear. Alex would often stumble around in the dim light, excitement bubbling inside him, while his father moved deliberately, his calm demeanor a poignant reminder of the serenity that waited at the water's edge.

"Patience is key, son," his father would whisper, tucking a baited hook onto the line with the precision of a surgeon. "It's not about how fast we catch the fish—it's about being in the moment and observing the world around us. You'll learn quickly that the best things often require time."

At first, Alex struggled with this concept. He was a young boy bursting with energy, eager for action and results. Sitting still for long stretches felt torturous, every ripple on the water igniting his anticipation. But under his father's watchful eye, he learned to find joy in the pauses, the stillness that characterized those bright, sun-soaked mornings. Every cast of the line became a lesson in itself, an invitation to enjoy the wait, to appreciate the conversations that flowed as easily as the gentle ripples on the lake's surface.

There was a particular day that stayed etched in Alex's memory—a day they spent building a small wooden model of a sailboat together. He was excited, having imagined countless adventures on the high seas, the thrill of waves crashing against the hull, and the fun of pretending to be a daring captain. Alex envisioned a quick and easy construction, but as they gathered the materials, his dreams of rapid progress rapidly transformed into frustration. The pieces refused to fit, the instructions became a blur of confusion, and before long, his eagerness morphed into a frown.

"Patience, my boy," Alex's father said softly, placing a hand on his shoulder as they sat on the porch, tools and wood scattered around them. "It's about the process, not just the finished product. Let's take our time."

So they sat there, focused together amidst the chaos of tools, laughter escaping their lips as they joked about their clumsy mistakes. They measured, cut, and sanded the wood diligently, as his father imparted nuggets of wisdom hidden within their shared labor. "Every mistake is a step toward growth, and every delay an opportunity to learn," he would say, encouraging Alex to embrace the lessons in every misstep.

The sun climbed higher, and the scent of sawdust mixed with fresh pine filled the air around them. It took longer than Alex had anticipated, but as they finally affixed the last piece—the mast—an overwhelming sense of accomplishment washed over him. That uneventful afternoon transformed into an unforgettable moment, illuminated by the laughter they shared, the memories etched in time through their patient efforts and the connection they forged.

Weeks later, as Alex found himself immersed in parenting, he couldn't shake the feeling that those lessons were far more significant than mere hobbies. They stamped ideas about connection deep within him, convictions about the importance of investing time in understanding not just the activity but his child, as well.

"Can we build something together, Dad?" Jamie asked one Saturday morning, eyes gleaming with possibility. The question lit a spark in Alex's heart, igniting memories of those gentle days spent with his father. It wasn't merely about constructing a tangible object; it was an opportunity to foster a bond, an avenue for nurturing Jamie's developing interests through the lens of patience.

"I'd love that, buddy! What do you want to build?"

As they rifled through materials in the garage, gathering wood, nails, and paint, Alex felt an exhilarating blend of nostalgia and responsibility. He wanted to be the kind of father who nurtured his child's creativity and curiosity without imposing the pressure of perfection.

"You know, Jamie, building isn't always about the end result. It's about enjoying the time we share and learning along the way." Alex smiled and glanced at Jamie, who watched him wide-eyed.

The project they ventured on became a makeshift treehouse—a lofty retreat where adventures could await, wild imaginations could run free, and where patient hands could mold dreams into reality. The two spent afternoons designing it, pouring over blueprints, and sketching possibilities. They laughed and played, amidst youthful banter, echoing the lessons Alex had learned.

In the early days, it was messy—wood was misaligned, screws went into the wrong spot, and blueprints got lost in the shuffle of excitement. But Alex gently guided Jamie through the moments of frustration, replicating the calm his father had instilled in him so long ago.

"Take your time, bud," Alex encouraged, kneeling beside him. "Let's fix it together. This is part of getting better!"

They shared snacks as they worked, their collaboration a seamless blend of joy and affection. With every mistake, with every rearrangement, Jamie absorbed patience as a way of life; he concluded that building was just as much about learning to navigate the ebbs and flows of creation as it was about the finished structure. They learned to communicate with trust, just as Alex had done with his father—their conversations marked with light-heartedness reinforced by love and understanding.

But it wasn't just those tangible projects that refined Alex's perspective on patience. During their favorite after-dinner walks, as they strolled through their neighborhood, Jamie would share every little observation: the size of the sunflowers, the way the clouds formed in shapes of dragons and castles, the peculiar barking of the neighbor's dog. At times, childhood queries spiraled into endless loops of "Why?" that could wear on any parent's patience.

“Why is the sky blue, Dad?” Jamie asked one evening, his intent gaze searching for answers that surpassed Alex’s rudimentary understanding of color and physics. Alex felt a swell of impatience creeping in, the urge to rush through the seemingly mundane question. But then he caught himself, remembering how his father would always take a moment, reflecting on his own understanding and simplifying the complexities without dismissing his son’s awe.

“Well, buddy, the sky looks blue because of how sunlight interacts with the atmosphere. But you know what? I don’t have all the answers. Let’s find out together!” This was a pivotal moment, not just for Jamie’s curiosity but for Alex’s own growth. They spent the rest of the evening looking up articles and watching educational videos on light, tracing the questions of the universe with laughter and inquiry. In nurturing curiosity, Alex was immortalizing his father’s zest for knowledge within Jamie—a bond growing as deep as any that could be forged through shared experiences alone.

As time rolled on, the treehouse stood completed, a testament not merely to wood, nails, and paint, but a reflection of their shared moments, trials, and lessons. More than once, Jamie would beckon for his friends to join them, and together they navigated adventures under the wooden canopy. As they played, Alex sat back and observed, a warmth blossoming in his heart. He knew that the patience they nurtured within that treehouse was woven into the fabric of Jamie’s lifetime.

"Hey, Dad," Jamie called out one afternoon, excitement coursing through him as he leapt from a wooden platform above. "Let's have a sailboat race next!"

Alex's heart surged at the idea, mirroring his own childhood memories. "That sounds great! Let's get some materials to build our boats!" He recalled the lessons of fishing and building sailing vessels with his own father, the joy anchored in the journey rather than the destination.

As they spent that evening creating tiny sailboats from scrap materials, Alex felt a liberating realization washing over him; patience had become a central tenet of his fatherhood, an ethos connecting generations amidst the ongoing transitions of life. These lessons were not confined to the confines of projects and play; patience carved lines that stretched into discipline and understanding—realities that echoed moments of vulnerability and heart to heart connections.

Through fishing trips, model building, outdoor endeavors, and casual conversations, the essence of patience unveiled itself—not merely as a practice of awaiting outcomes but as a powerful foundation supporting the expectations of connection. Alex's relationship with Jamie grew to reflect the very values his father had instilled years ago, creating a legacy where love occupied center stage, providing nourishment to minds hungry for understanding.

But Alex knew, even with all the integration of his father's lessons, that fatherhood was no linear path. Encouragement had its shadows—days when impatience would rear its head, when fatigue clashed with passion, and moments of doubt loomed across his horizon. But it was in recognizing his vulnerabilities that he preserved the nurturing spirit his father imparted; the same warmth cultivated years ago vibrated through their relationship.

On a particularly testing afternoon, amid emotional upheavals as Jamie struggled with homework and Alex battled fatigue from the demands of work, a conversation spiraled into an emotional landscape. "Why can't I get this right?" Jamie cried out, frustration peering through his eyes. Alex felt the tension rising, but just as the shadows threatened to swallow the light, he paused, drawing on the well of patience his father had taught him.

With deep breaths, he knelt beside Jamie, his heart open, ready to navigate these turbulent waters together. "It's alright, Jamie. Everyone struggles sometimes. Let's break it down. We can do this together, just like my dad helped me with the things I found tough." In that moment, the very essence of connection over performance took root, open dialogues seeded with trust, understanding, and vulnerability paving the path forward.

As Alex looked back, navigating through the spectrum of lessons baptism by love, he reflected on each encounter—fishing, building, and simply being present. The patient instilling of those values wasn't just a passing gift; it had the potential to shape, mold, and light a path for generations to come.

As evening settled, he and Jamie embraced in a beaming light of recognition, knowing that their bond was stronger than the challenges ahead. Alex smiled, watching his son grow—an individual full of curiosity—confident that the values passed down would echo through the years. The journey of patience was woven intricately into their very existence, a timeless thread guiding them forward in the adventure of fatherhood where love flourished in the heart of every decision.

Ultimately, it's in that patience, that investment of genuine time and belief in connection, that allows little moments to evolve into lasting memories, shaping their journey together against the backdrop of the ever-changing tapestry of life.

The Roots of Nurturing

As Alex reflected on his childhood, a tapestry of memories wove itself into a vivid narrative. This narrative was rich with lessons—moments that burgeoned with the laughter of familial love, the shared struggle of understanding, and the tender caress of nurturing spirits that would guide him into fatherhood. The lessons were not always spoken; often, they lingered in the air, behind the warmth of a hug or the glimmer of his father's eyes as they shared simple yet profound moments of connection.

Alex's earliest memories took him to a sun-drenched backyard, where laughter danced among the trees. His father often engaged him in play, inviting him into worlds fueled by imagination. It was in those playful moments that Alex first learned lessons of compassion. Whether they were building intricate fortresses from colorful blocks or exploring the boundless wonders of their small garden, every interaction was laced with encouragement.

“Let's build it bigger, Alex! What do you think we could add to make it even more special?” his father would ask, drawing the boy into a blend of creativity and teamwork.

These early interactions taught Alex that collaboration, rather than competition, formed the core of understanding. As they built together, his father fostered not just a sense of achievement but also a gentle acknowledgment that ideas flow better when shared.

He learned that compassion drives human connection, showing early on that parenting is about nurturing potential.

On rainy days when they couldn't venture outdoors, his father pulled out their trusty board games, proposing a friendly rivalry that thrummed with excitement. Winning was secondary to strategizing together, laughing at perceived blunders, and celebrating each success. The air was thick with shared joy, but it was the way his father lost that resonated most deeply.

"Winning isn't everything, Alex. Sometimes, just having fun matters more," he would say, patting his son on the back.

In those moments, Alex internalized the idea that being a good father meant finding joy in the journey rather than focusing strictly on the outcome. The empathy displayed through his father's playful guidance influenced his belief in staying connected amid the ebb and flow of life's ups and downs.

As Alex transitioned to school, the multifaceted layers of understanding continued to deepen. His father often taught him that words bore weight and that conversations acted as building blocks for relationships. His nurturing nature consistently encouraged open dialogue, affording Alex the courage to express his thoughts while allowing him to navigate the myriad complexities of friendships.

"Talk it out," his father would say. "Don't keep it bottled inside. The words don't just help others understand you; they help you understand yourself."

These precious nuggets of wisdom rippled through his experiences, reinforcing that emotional awareness fortified connections. Each moment spent discussing school challenges, friendships, and fears equipped Alex with the tools necessary to navigate life's intricate web of relationships. More importantly, it instilled the belief that vulnerability was not a weakness; rather, it was an invitation for others to meet him in a place of shared humanity.

As childhood morphed into adolescence, Alex faced the tumult of teenage years—a time when insecurities could easily overwhelm the strongest of spirits. It dawned on him that his father's nurturing presence was a steadfast anchor amid storms of uncertainty. Late-night chats often revolved around fears of acceptance and ambitions that seemed grand yet distant.

"Dad, what if I don't fit in?" he once asked, his voice breaking under the weight of adolescent angst. His father turned to him, eyes softening, exuding a warmth that seemed to envelop Alex in a cocoon of reassurance.

"Fitting in isn't about changing who you are; it's about finding those who appreciate the uniqueness you bring," his father replied.

Those words resonated deeply within Alex. They shaped his perception of identity, instilling a belief that authenticity fosters connections far beyond superficial friendships. He learned about honoring one's essence and embracing his own narrative as a pathway to self-acceptance.

In those formative years, Alex encountered pivotal moments where his father modeled resilience and understanding—traits that he would carry forward into his interpretation of fatherhood. There were episodes of personal frustration, setbacks, and the occasional heartbreak that put his father's nurturing methods to the test, yet each situation was met with unwavering support.

During a particularly difficult time when Alex faced rejection from a crush, he locked himself in his room, engulfed in the heaviness of disappointment. A soft knock on the door interrupted his spiraling thoughts. When he emerged, his father was waiting, armed with a tray of snacks and a story ready to be shared.

"Let me tell you about my first crush," he began, a warm smile dancing upon his lips. Over laughter and shared memories, Alex learned that love could be painful yet beautiful—a nuance of life he now embraced with open arms. His father's ability to normalize heartbreak illustrated the strength in vulnerability, a lesson he would carry forward into his own parenting style.

As Alex journeyed into young adulthood, he became increasingly aware of how ingrained these nurturing lessons shaped his perception of love, compassion, and understanding. His father exemplified the profound role of emotional intelligence, emphasizing the importance of relationships over accolades. With graduation looming, the lessons solidified into his identity—a mold now hardened with experiences of acceptance and love.

With his father's guidance, Alex actively sought opportunities to extend these lessons beyond the walls of their home. He volunteered at local shelters, sharing stories and providing companionship to children who had faced immense challenges. There, his father's spirit echoed vibrantly, reinforcing the belief that humanity thrived in compassion. The connection established through shared laughter became a nurturing catalyst, paving the way for everyday miracles of change.

Those interactions illuminated Alex's understanding that nurturing was not confined to familial dynamics—it was a broader tapestry woven through human connection. Every smile offered, every encouragement given, every moment of compassion reflected the tender roots his father had planted within him.

As he transitioned into fatherhood himself, Alex's heart brimmed with old lessons reawakened. The building blocks garnered through those formative years now guided his instinctual responses toward his son. Each time he embraced his child, it echoed the gentle embrace of his father—a promise to support and instill an atmosphere of confidence and loss-free exploration.

“Let's build something amazing together,” Alex often told his son, the long shadow of his father drifting along beside them. His nurturing spirit emerged not as a mere echo but as a symphony—a continuation of the love and lessons passed down through generations.

In the soft glow of dawn, as he watched his son delve into imaginative play, Alex felt the full weight of nurturing's legacy. The roots planted during his own childhood nourished the budding relationship with his son, weaving a narrative rich in empathy, understanding, and shared joy.

Through the stories and lessons of his father, he recognized the intricate dance of love—the embrace of vulnerability tethered to strength, the value of connection forged through empathy, and the joy of simply being present. It was a beautiful legacy that blossomed like wildflowers, guiding Alex on the remarkable journey of fatherhood. As the days unfolded, he marveled at how these roots had formed a tree, its branches extending wide enough to envelop a new generation in the warm embrace of nurturing.

In those reflective moments, Alex fully grasped the essence of nurturing: it was an art guided by the tender hands of experience, painted with hues of compassion and love. It was about offering understanding amid life's chaos and wrapping moments of vulnerability in unwavering acceptance. Those very roots had shaped him into the father he aspired to be, a father determined to carve out a nurturing space for his child—a space where love would always reign supreme.

The Iron Hand in Velvet Gloves

A Different Kind of Love

The sun hung low in the sky, casting long shadows on the polished hardwood floor of the gym as the boys gathered for another rigorous basketball practice. The gym echoed with a cacophony of sneakers squeaking against the surface, punctuated by the sharp twang of the ball hitting the ground. Alex watched from the sidelines, a silent observer navigating the turmoil of emotions stirred by his best friend's world. While he embraced the warmth of his own father's nurturing guidance, he found himself peering into the austere environment from which Jake emerged.

Jake's world was ruled by the looming figure of his father, a retired athlete who sought to impose his own aspirations onto his son with an iron grip. It was a world molded by rigidity, where every moment felt orchestrated, every setback a personal affront. As Alex observed the tension on Jake's brow during practice, he felt the familiar pang of concern—a pang he often pushed aside, unwilling to intrude on the complexities of Jake's life.

The coach's voice shattered the air, punctuated by sharp commands that resonated through the gym like an authoritative drumbeat. "Pay attention! You call that a play? I expect more from you!" Each word bore the weight of expectation, reverberating through the hearts of the young athletes scrambling to meet the high standards set before them. But Alex knew it was different for Jake; he felt the palpable pressure to excel, to ride the waves of his father's relentless demands.

Late afternoons spent together, talking about their day, felt like a gentle contrast. Back then, Alex often found solace in their conversations, deftly avoiding the harsher realities of Jake's home life. They were young kids, reveling in the freedom of childhood, yet lurking beneath the surface was a silent understanding of how different their worlds truly were. Alex remembered sitting cross-legged on the floor of his bedroom, sharing dreams with Jake, unaware that those dreams were burdensome for Jake when he returned home.

A pivotal moment from those practices lingered vividly in Alex's mind—an incident so striking it felt etched into the fabric of their childhood. It was a day when everything coalesced, merging intensity and desperation into a single moment of clarity. The boys were scheduled to scrimmage against their rival team, the air crackling with anticipation. The stakes felt high, almost too high for boys so young, yet Jake's father had crafted the narrative—this game could define the boy!

As the scrimmage commenced, the sound of the ball echoed like a heartbeat in the gym. Jake, fueled by adrenaline, moved deftly along the court, his focus unwavering. Alex could see the fire in his friend's eyes, a testament to the hours spent drilling plays under the steely gaze of his father. But with each dribble, with every shot, a haunting shadow trailed behind—a fear of inadequacy that loomed larger than life.

During one pivotal moment, Jake seized the ball from a defender, darting towards the basket with a swift determination. The crowd erupted, exhilaration filling the air as he took flight, soaring toward the hoop. Time seemed to suspend as he reached for the rim, but in that instant, the unforgiving hand of fate intervened. A thunderous collision echoed through the gym as Jake came crashing down, the impact leaving him gasping for breath.

Silence enveloped the court as everyone rushed to check on him. The coach's face twisted in concern, while players surrounded Jake, their eyes filled with a mixture of fear and care. But in the distance, behind that moment of chaos, stood Jake's father, his expression hard as stone. Instead of rushing to his son's side, he shouted, "Get up! You're not hurt! Stop limping and play!" His words echoed, resonating with an authority that sought to overshadow all else.

Alex felt the sting of indignation pulse within him. First aid kits and grounding techniques were pointless in this moment—what Jake needed was not just acknowledgment of his physical pain, but empathy for the sheer emotional toll that discipline exacted on him. As Jake struggled to regain his footing, Alex saw something dim in his friend's spirit—a flicker that extinguished under the weight of vulnerability stripped bare.

It didn't go unnoticed by the rest of the team. There was a silence, a momentary pause where compassion battled the sonorous commands from Jake's father. Jake's shoulders slumped for an instant, a gesture unnoticed by the adults yet profoundly felt by Alex—an indication of the invisible scars that shaped Jake's being. How often had they laughed, how often had they shared moments of triumph only to be overshadowed by the specter of rigid expectations?

Through that layer of anxiety, Alex realized a different kind of love governed Jake's life: one that thrived in the tension between success and emotional warmth. It was a tough-love philosophy imprinted in the very essence of Jake's home, where the idea of affection twisted into something far less accessible. The adrenaline rush of victory often came at the cost of hidden suffering, and Alex felt the awareness like a piercing arrow in his chest.

As the game resumed, Jake's movements grew cautious. Though his body took to the court with practiced skill, the spark of joy that once illuminated his face began to fade. He no longer played for the thrill of the game; he played under scrutiny—an ever-watchful eye demanding excellence without fail. As Alex watched, he felt an urgency bubbling within him, a yearning to reach out and shake Jake from the shadows that cloaked him. Yet he hesitated—concerned that crossing the unspoken lines of their friendship would fracture the already tenuous bond they shared.

Practices continued in the months that followed, each session a reminder of the dichotomy between their childhoods. While Alex thrived in the warmth of encouragement from his father, Jake was shackled under the weight of expectation. The experiences at the gym became a painful tapestry woven with threads of victory and defeat, joy and anxiety. Each time Jake fell short, it felt as though he lost a piece of himself, a piece swallowed by the void of unattainable perfection.

The barbecues at Alex's house became refuge points. He could hear the laughter resonating from the backyard, the aroma of burgers wafting through the air as their fathers shared stories of their own childhood, unaware of the dynamic unraveling in their sons. The contrast between Alex's father and Jake's began to weigh heavily on Alex's shoulders—he wanted to shield Jake, but felt paralyzed by the ritual of boyhood bonding. He loved the simplicity of joy fostered in his home, and it made witnessing Jake's struggles all the more heartrending.

Jake often looked to the ground, lost in thoughts too heavy for a boy of his age. For every compliment he deserved from the coach, every moment of grace, there was the shadow of his father's disappointment lurking nearby. The silent expectation seeped through their conversations—every shared moment tinged with the unspoken heaviness of competitiveness. A kind word felt almost blasphemous in the wake of that rigid upbringing, and Alex occasionally found himself choking on the words he longed to say.

It soon became apparent that Jake's internal struggles reached beyond basketball; they shaped his interactions in and out of school. While Alex reveled in confidence, Jake navigated life as a prisoner to the ideal his father created. The cycle continued; each time he succeeded, the victory was marred by the race to do more—to achieve higher—to win at the cost of connection. Over time, the once vibrant spark in Jake's laugh dimmed as he slipped further away from the carefree joy they once shared, encased in a hardened shell shaped by relentless discipline.

Compassion often swirled within Alex, but words clung to his throat like a scroll sealed with invisible ink—the meaning buried beneath layers of societal expectations. Each time he tried to mentor Jake through the trauma of high standards, he felt lost, a voice rendered mute in the face of heartbreaking realities.

One afternoon, as they shared pizza and soda in Alex's living room, the tension broke in an unexpected confession. The light-hearted banter shifted into heavier air as Jake opened up about his father's expectations. “You know, sometimes I feel like I'm just an extension of his failed dreams, like I can never be enough,” he admitted, gaze locked to the floor as he pushed a piece of pepperoni around on his plate.

For the first time, vulnerability spilled open like a cracked shell—Jake's honesty cutting through the barrier of their friendship. Alex sat in stunned reverence, unsure of how to respond. It struck him then just how deeply the pressure weighed on his friend.

“I'm not like you, Alex—my dad doesn't just want me to be good; he wants me to be the best. And if I fail, it feels like I let him down every time,” Jake's voice trembled with the weight of those words.

A familiar rage boiled within Alex, masking the sadness he felt for the experience Jake faced daily.

“Man—I hate that for you. It shouldn't be like that. You're amazing, you're talented! You shouldn't have to compete with what someone else assesses as good enough,” Alex said, passion boiling in his voice, trying to provide a warmth that seeped through the coldness prevailing in Jake's world.

Jake merely shrugged as the shadows fell across his face, feeling the pull of his father's harsh love linger between them, undiscriminating and dense. “You don't understand,” he replied softly. "It's not just basketball—this is it. The pressure is everywhere. It's all about what I can accomplish to earn the love." The admission settled between them, heavy like an anchor that anchored their friendship in deeper waters.

As days turned to weeks and seasons shifted, that pivotal practice melded itself into Alex's understanding of love—a complex blend of tenderness amidst toughness—the notion that loving through discipline can sometimes cloud the essence of love entirely. Jake became a mirror reflecting fear back at Alex, reminding him that the line between love and control often blurred, creating wounds that ran deeper than any physical pain endured.

In Alex's own home, he began perceiving softness more than perfection—an understanding that building a life centered on nurturing demanded space for others to thrive, to falter, and to learn without the looming shadows of harsh expectations. Jake's journey reframed his vision of fatherhood, forcing him to reconcile aspects of his own upbringing with the echo of his father's touch—a warm embrace juxtaposed against the dissonant demands heard through Jake's world.

And so, in this delicate composition of friendship, love, and growth, Alex understood something profound—each style of parenting bore its own complexities. The iron hand may yield strength, but the velvet glove was where connection blossomed.

As he continued to support Jake in both triumph and trials, Alex learned to hold space as a brother—instead of seeking to shield him from pain, he became a steadfast presence. A bridge connecting the worlds of warmth and discipline, growing together in the rhythm of life's lessons. In this friendship, amid the shadows and light, he discovered a different kind of love—one tempered by understanding, patience, and presence in the face of unyielding expectations.

The Cost of Rigor

The Cost of Rigor

Every family carries its stories, each woven tightly into the fabric of their existence, yet none are as haunting to Alex as the tale of his best friend, Jake. Growing up just a stone's throw away from each other, their lives were intertwining threads in the same tapestry; however, the colors of their family environments were starkly different. Where Alex experienced the warmth of summer sun in his nurturing family, Jake's upbringing felt more like the chill of an unforgiving winter, marked by the iron fist of his father, a man whose fierce commitment to discipline often overshadowed the love that pulsed beneath it. This constant contrast haunted Alex, casting shadows on his own understanding of what it meant to be a father.

As a child, Jake was always driven, his father's rigorous expectations setting him on a path of ambition from an early age. Alex remembered how Jake's home was often shrouded in a palpable tension, a quiet weight that pressed down on the walls like the gray clouds that sometimes came rolling into the neighborhood. The high-pitched voice of Jake's father would cut through the air like a razor, dissecting the joy often found in childhood with brutal critiques about practice and perseverance. “You call that a throw? You're better than that!” his father would bark during their little league games. Each word was as heavy as a stone, and Alex often wondered how Jake managed to carry the load.

In contrast, Alex's home was a sanctuary where love and encouragement flowed freely. His father's soft-spoken praise acted as a soothing balm against insecurity, empowering him to embrace exploration, to understand that mistakes were intrinsically woven into the fabric of growth. “It’s okay to fail, son. You learn more from mistakes than from successes,” he would say, casually spinning off a reassuring smile that cradled Alex's burgeoning spirit. This philosophy greatly impacted how Alex perceived the world, allowing him the freedom to navigate life’s challenges with resilience.

But in Jake’s world, failure wasn't merely accepted—it was met with disappointment. Alex saw it happen time and again. Each time Jake slipped from perfection, the air would grow heavier, and the warmth in his father’s presence would evaporate. Alex could feel it too, the way Jake seemed to shrink in on himself, a flower wilting under a relentless sun.

“Jake, what did you do wrong? You are better than this. You let your team down!” The sharp words hung like a storm cloud over Jake’s head, threatening to unleash rain upon his fragile confidence. It dawned on Alex that Jake had no safety net; there was no embrace to catch him in his moments of vulnerability. Instead, every mistake seemed to deepen the chasm between him and his father—a chasm skirted with unspoken words and unmet expectations, an abyss that consumed the boy's spirit in its relentless pursuit of perfection.

The nights Alex spent crashing at Jake’s house always resonated with the ambient sound of tension. The walls seemed to carry whispers of discontent and the faint rustle of disappointment that would creep into the edges of their conversations. One night, he witnessed a pivotal moment that would haunt him in the depths of his parenting journey. It was a Tuesday, and the fading light prickled through the curtains as Jake’s father returned home, the weight of the world with him. Unbeknownst to Alex, the day had been marked by a poor performance at a math competition, an event where Jake, under his usual pressures, had faltered.

When Jake mentioned his day, he was met with a gaze that seemed to hold storms—his father's disappointment manifesting in an icy silence that pulled down the atmosphere of the room. "You know," his father began, voice low and laced with an intensity that sliced through the fabric of their camaraderie, "wasting time on distractions won't get you anywhere. You want to be someone? Then start acting like it." The importance of success had shifted from an encouragement for Jake to thrive to a guillotine dangling over his head, executing dreams of adequacy with every slip.

This singular moment of realization cut deep, and Alex found his throat tightening as he felt the emotional distance that had formed between Jake and his father. Each communication was transactional; devoid of warmth, instead laden with demands. Alex felt a rising tide of anger and sorrow as he watched the boy he cared for fade a little more under the weight of expectations placed upon him, turning him into a shadow of his former self—a kaleidoscope of unfulfilled promises and aching strife.

In those fleeting years of childhood bliss, what had once been a friendship filled with laughter was rapidly morphing into a shared silence punctuated by the echoes of critique and the absence of comfort. Alex often found himself wrestling with worry for Jake, whose spirit appeared to shatter slightly more with each passing reprimand. It was a warning sign, a cautionary tale interwoven into the very fabric of their lives.

As the years rolled on, the suffocating hands of rigid expectations tightened their grip around Jake's heart, altering its rhythm. Alex would often note how pressure morphed into fear, fear into anxiety, and anxiety into a tide of emotional distance that left Jake isolated in a swirling calm of guilt and inadequacy. The myriad of achievements accumulated over the years began to feel hollow, coated with a veneer of success created not out of joy, but from fear of punishment lurking in the background.

At school, Jake excelled—his report cards gleaming with gold stars that served as trophies of his relentless pursuit for approval. But there was an underlying sadness in each praise he received, a joy dampened by the haunting whispers of impending disappointment. Alex could sense how Jake's victories were moments of fleeting joy; after each accomplishment came the inevitable assessment—was it enough? Every accolade was weighed against the austere standards set by a father whose love came shrouded in limits, creating a precarious effort to gauge worth.

Conversations turned into examinations, and laughter into regrets as Jake's responses shifted from youthful exuberance to a stilted formality. As they grew older, the cracks began to show through, the cost of rigor revealing its dire price. Jake's laughter, once infectious and full of life, sounded increasingly hollow in the echo of restrained excitement, muffled under the dense fog of unreal influence.

Then there came the day when, after yet another stringent evaluation from his father, Jake confided in Alex: "I don't think I'm ever gonna be good enough." A shiver ran down Alex's spine; the words were sharp, cutting through their adolescent dreams, a haunting specter that Alex learned to dread. The statement burrowed deep within his thoughts and solidified the warnings he would carry with him into fatherhood.

“I can’t disappoint him,” said Jake, the tremor in his voice resonating deeply with Alex's own fears. “Every time I think I’m doing well, he finds a way to let me know that I could do better. I just want him to be proud of me.” It became clear then how recorded achievements morph into burdens—Jake’s spiraling hopes formed marionette strings tied directly to his father’s approval.

As the years passed, Alex often found himself reflecting on the sense of emotional distance leaving Jake stranded in a void between his father’s expectations and his own desires. A heaviness brewed deep in Alex’s chest, for he had witnessed a soul crushed under the rigors of performance, and he could already feel the burden it placed on him as a future father. If rigid discipline could shatter Jake's spirit, how close was he to feeling that weight in his own parenting?

The memories of Jake would surface—always painted in excruciating detail. That moment spent in their high school, when Jake stood alone in a hallway facing the wall, surrounded by the mundane chatter of teenage life. The laughter and joy irked him, a mocking reminder of the connections he felt were beyond his reach. In that stark isolation, Alex stepped in, extending a hand, desperate to bridge the distance that had sprung forth. “You’re still you, regardless of that gradesheet,” he reminded him gently, “You’re worth more than the numbers.” Yet, Jake remained unconvinced. Each refusal to accept affection layered on the emotional distance, wedging their friendship into uncomfortable spaces marked by the need for approval.

The reality of the cost of rigor settled in Alex like an unsettling weight, echoing through the hallowed halls of his heart. The deep-rooted implications of Jake's upbringing filled him with anxiety.

As he stood in front of his own son, Alexander, he felt the echoes of Jake's struggles whispering cautions—warnings of past failures that rang loudly in his ears. What if he, too, fell into the trap of demanding too much? Would he find himself emulating his friend's father's harshness? The very thoughts sent chills skittering down his spine like tiny shards of ice.

Watching Alexander explore the world with wide-eyed wonder, Alex felt a deep, instinctual desire to nurture his son's spirit, to allow him the chance to fail and rise again, unshackled by unyielding expectations. In those vulnerable years, beneath the surface of gleeful laughter, Alex wanted nothing more than to shield his son from rigidity's punishing embrace.

The memory of Jake—his fears, his storm of inadequacy—served as both a warning and a lesson, a mathematical equation filled with variables of love and anguish. Even the brightest successes, Alex realized, were often tainted by existential uncertainty, a specter of a past that whispered from the shadows of every achievement. Would his son face a similar plight, caught in the tightening grip of the iron hand disguised within velvet gloves?

The specters of regret haunted him frequently. The realization that Jake's life could have been sculpted differently under a gentler hand, where a nurturing father descended instead of a tyrannical ruler. With each day that passed, Alex steeled his resolve to ensure that his son would never experience the same heavy burdens that so nearly crushed the spirit of his dear friend. No more would he mirror the harshness painted in the lines of Jake's life; he would instead create a refuge bathed in warmth and respect, where mistakes could blossom into learned lessons.

As Alex embraced the delicate dance between nurturing and discipline, he also grappled with the instinctual fears that arose from witnessing the cost of rigor. To love was to create an unbreakable bond, not one wrought from chains of expectation. In his reflections, he found clarity, vowing never to let the specters of regret dictate the future of their shared journey.

Armed with the wisdom gained from the echoes of his past friendship, Alex decided to embrace a gentler approach, actively redefining the paradigm of fatherhood for himself. The specter of Jake's story would remain a constant reminder, a guide carved from the vulnerability of friendship fraught with hardship. Through the intricate interplay of love and discipline, Alex embarked on a mission to create a nurturing environment for Alexander that fostered exploration over evaluation, to craft a legacy saturated in the gentle warmth he once experienced himself.

And as evening settled in, accompanied by the sounds of laughter dancing effortlessly among shadows, Alex took a deep breath, nurturing not just his son's growth, but the decidedly softer path he avowed to tread—a path illuminated by understanding that the cost of love must always strive to outweigh the cost of rigor.

An Emerging Conflict

The sun hung low in the sky, casting long shadows across the playfield where Alex and his son, Jamie, were finishing up their Saturday afternoon routine. Squeals of laughter and the soft thud of a basketball echoed from nearby courts, but Alex's attention was caught by the sharp whistle of a coach that pierced the air like a sudden crack of thunder. It belonged to Denny, his best friend, whose imposing figure drifted across the courts where a dozen eager teenagers hustled to perfect their skills. Denny's father, a man of few words but endless expectations, continued to loom in the back of Alex's mind as he watched Jamie squeak across the pavement, chasing after a rogue soccer ball.

For years, Denny's father embodied authority—a towering presence who believed that rigidity fostered resilience. Discipline folded neatly into the fabric of his parenting, a thick cloth woven from the threads of tough love. As Alex observed Jamie clumsily manage to bring the soccer ball under his control, memories surged forth from his own childhood, fractured yet vivid—among them, moments spent in Denny's household, where each mistake felt magnified under the pressure of scrutiny.

At first, Alex had felt admiration for Denny's father. The man demanded excellence, instilling a sort of reverence in Alex's young heart—a belief that grit and perseverance could carve achievements from thin air. But as Alex revisited these memories, something within him stirred—a gut-wrenching realization that chilled his admiration. Denny had been molded under that strict approach, yet what had been gained came at a cost.

Denny's jocular demeanor often masked the weight of his upbringing, the emotional distance from a father who praised victory but seldom recognized the vulnerability that accompanied failure. In moments of reflection, Alex recognized that the disciplined upbringing had not only crafted Denny into a resilient young athlete but had also formed an unyielding wall that often stood between them, a boundary marked by the silence of unexpressed fears and unacknowledged feelings.

As he watched Jamie giggle in triumph over a successful kick, Alyx felt a wave of conflict wash over him. The question pressed at the back of his mind: could he shield his child from the same fate?

"Are you going to join us, or just stand there?" Denny's voice sliced through the clouds of Alex's thoughts, jolting him back to reality. He looked over to see Denny beckoning him with a playful grin, a teasing indication as he hoisted the soccer ball high.

"I'm on it," Alex replied, his voice betraying uncertainty.

As he joined Denny and the boys in their soccer match, the playful banter masked the tension building within him. Unlike Denny's father, Alex wanted to nurture patience and understanding in Jamie, creating a sanctuary where failure was not synonymous with shame. Yet the sugary rhetoric of support felt tested in Denny's presence—echoes of the old love-blueprint hovered within him like specters, creating an unbearable heaviness.

Each time Jamie missed a shot or stumbled while dribbling, Alex instinctively felt his heart race. Denny, while striving to teach the boys resilience, would bark instructions or critique every play with a practiced edge; a way of sharpening their skills. And Alex remained caught in the crosshairs of admiration and concern, marveling at Denny's ferocity while fretting over the implications of such harsh teaching.

"Focus, Jamie!" Denny's voice boomed across the field, snapping Alex's head around sharply.

Alex felt the sharp pang of apprehension shoot through him. The tone struck him; it rang familiar but wrong, reminiscent of Denny's father more than any fatherhood ideal Alex sought to embody. He could feel an uninvited seed of doubt germinating in his mind. Was Denny's approach something that could inspire, or was it merely a method of planting ideas of inadequacy?

As if sensing his internal turmoil, Jamie turned and caught Alex's eye, a flicker of uncertainty rippling across his brow as he froze mid-play. The innocence that radiated from him hit Alex with the weight of a realization—his son was not a vessel to be filled with critique and harsh discipline; he was a young spirit in need of encouragement and a safe space to explore his potential.

In that moment, Alex made a conscious decision—a shift in his intentions as Jamie's keeper. He approached his son, crouching down to meet his eyes, and spoke gently, "Hey buddy, remember that it's all about having fun, right? You're doing great."

Jamie's face brightened, and he quickened his pace, revitalized by the encouragement. It was a simple exchange, yet it marked the moment Alex recognized the flaw in the stricter approaches he had mostly absorbed from Denny's world. The fear was still there, nagging at the corners of his mind—fear of inadequacy as both a father and a friend, burdened by the memories of witnessing Denny's struggles and triumphs under his father's fist of discipline.

As the afternoon wore on, Alex felt the pinch of conflict deepen in his heart. He yearned to be the father who fused kindness with firmness—a blend of nurturing and necessary discipline—as he worked to create special moments in Jamie's upbringing without undermining the lessons that life inevitably carries.

Later, as evening descended, Alex sat at his kitchen table opposite his wife, Emma, pouring over notes about children's psychology he had been reading; research he felt he needed to re-arm himself for these parenting hurdles. He began to articulate the complexity of his thoughts, tracing their roots back to the soccer match. "I worry, Em. I saw Denny's approach today—he really pushes those kids—but I wonder what the cost is. I want to avoid the pitfalls we'll encounter if I'm too soft, but I don't think harshness is a remedy either."

Emma lifted an eyebrow, her expression a mixture of empathy and support. "You've seen it firsthand and felt it too. It's not enough to mimic someone else's way of parenting. You're not Denny, and Jamie isn't him. He's a different kid, and you have the power to raise him differently. You can show him the value of effort without making him feel like a failure."

Her voice resonated in the air, simmering in Alex's mind. As a child, he had lived through Denny's world—a world skewed by perceptions of success and failure, rough and tender moments—he wanted Jamie to navigate a different reality. The warmth of Emma's encouragement wrapped around him like a comforting blanket, softening the edges of his burdens.

The conversation carved deeper fissures of reflection, cascading into the shadows of his memories, ultimately illuminating a truth he could no longer ignore: discipline and love could coexist without conflict but only if they were blended mindfully, intentionally, with a merging of patience and kindness.

The following day, Alex decided to put his thoughts into action. After failing to help Jamie complete a puzzle, which had turned into a major temper tantrum, he sat with Jamie on the floor instead of opting for the traditional method of taking away his privileges. Instead, he pulled Jamie close, showed him the pieces and demonstrated, explaining as he went. He was excited when Jamie managed to fit two pieces together, and immediately enough Jamie's face lit up, a brief smile breaking through the tension.

"See? That's the way! You did it!" Alex exclaimed, filled with an urge to celebrate Jamie's small successes. A small victory for a curious little boy of four, but one that cemented a pivotal truth for Alex: collaboration didn't need to outweigh correction.

As he navigated the delicate balance of parenting, he began aligning each choice with love—a concentrated effort to guide rather than critique. It was during this chapter of stepping into uncharted waters that Alex recognized a practical truth: the importance of instilling discipline framed by affection.

Back at the playfield, during another Saturday afternoon with Denny, Alex approached Jamie again when he showed signs of frustration during practice. This time, his intervention came preemptively, and he knelt beside Jamie. "You seem a little frustrated. Remember, it's perfectly all right to miss; nobody's perfect. We're here to grow together."

The curve of Jamie's joyous laughter filled the clearing, penetrating the air thick with competition. It was richer than any echo of Denny's voice from past matches, and for the first time, he realized the difference was palpable.

Denny, untouched by the change that had settled into Alex's heart, continued to bark orders from a distance, reinforcing the stringent rules of engagement on the field. But Alex noticed the heavy fog of discontent that hovered over the boys responding to his friend's commands. The playful essence of youth felt at odds with Denny's no-nonsense tone, which prompted Alex to lean in closer to this burgeoning divide.

In witnessing Denny's rigid outlines create barriers among the players, Alex gained clarity; the gap was growing bigger. He felt empowered, no longer dragged down by the admiration for Denny's methods—now, he found himself actively seeking a new amalgam rooted in empathy, reflecting the softness of his upbringing and the powerful impact that love could have even amidst discipline.

It was after one of these sessions that Denny, leaning against the fence post, commented, "I don't get how you do it, Alex. You're too soft, man. Kids need to know they can't get everything handed to them."

Alex chose his words thoughtfully. "I believe kids can learn without fear of judgment. There's a fine line between pushing them too hard and supporting them through challenges."

Denny just shrugged it off, a flicker of bemusement lingering in his eyes. Clearly, the years spent growing up in opposition to his father's lessons had led him to believe that a hard exterior was a mark of strength—one Alex no longer intended to follow.

The evolving dynamic became apparent in subsequent weeks. Jamie began to express himself in new ways. He was less afraid to share his failures, looking for ways to problem-solve without fear of criticism. Alex's heart swelled with pride as his son learned resilience built on love rather than avoidance.

Through this process, Alex recognized how the tension was not only between him and Denny but echoed within himself, alighting a deeper struggle for understanding his role as a father. The realization that a balance had to be struck between firmness and warmth gave Alex a platform from which to spring; a transformative view blossomed within him. Five words emerged to guide him: "Love, understand, support, teach, and grow."

As weeks turned into months, the once-dissonant echoes of conflict began receding into an encompassing harmony. In moments of correction or discipline, Alex infused his love into the lesson, moving beyond the narrow confines of legacy to forge a fresh path rooted in empathy.

His relationship with Jamie flourished due to Alex's reflective practices—for every mistake corrected, he lined the lesson with encouragement. There appeared a new win-win dimension where accountability and warmth connected, bringing forth the realization that love could and should fuel even the more challenging interactions of raising a child.

Ultimately, in those quiet moments when the shadows of prior conflicts floated back, Alex clung to his renewed understanding: the heart of parenting lies not in one philosophy over another but in crafting an approach that speaks to the unique essence of both child and parent.

Denny remained a constant presence, still wrapped in the embrace of expectations that seemed to obscure the possibility of warmth. But Alex had unearthed a path that honored the nurturing embrace of patience while still imparting crucial lessons of life—his determination to forge ahead was unwavering.

The emerging conflict both in and around him had catalyzed a profound evolution; one where tenderness truly reigned alongside the discipline needed to carve success with love, an honest balance perfect for the journey ahead. Ultimately, it was clear that he would not only embrace love but flourish in the wisdom gained—an undying commitment to a model of fatherhood that breathed life into both firmness and gentleness.

Caught in the Middle

The First Year of Parenthood

The house was filled with the sounds of life, a constant hum of activity that seemed to ebb and flow with the rhythms of a toddler exploring the vastness of his small world. Alex often found himself standing in the middle of it all, a rare mixture of chaos and joy swirling around him. In these early days of fatherhood, the dichotomous nature of his upbringing weighed heavily on his mind. Like a balancing act performed by a jester on a tightrope, he felt the pressure of parenting choices press against his chest, a constant reminder of the paths not yet taken.

As the sun streamed through the open windows, Alex cast a glance across the living room, cluttered with toys, stuffed animals, and the remnants of a breakfast that had been interrupted by the spontaneous wanderings of his son, Sam. The boy was barely a year old but already exhibited an unquenchable curiosity. Today, he was fixated on a brightly colored ball, gripping it with both hands, eyes wide with wonder as he pushed it across the floor, bewildered at the way it rolled and danced under his touch.

"Look at you go!" Alex encouraged, his voice a mix of excitement and pride. The words echoed in his heart, reminding him of his father's gentle praises during his own formative years. He could almost hear the soft timbre of his dad's encouragement, each syllable wrapped in warmth. In those fleeting moments, he understood not just the significance of the words but the intention behind them—a nurturing spirit meant to embolden.

Yet, another voice lingered at the back of his mind, a sharply defined standard—a strictness instilled by his best friend's father. The memories were stark and unforgiving. There was a time when Alex watched through the window of his friend's house, where discipline created an atmosphere laden with pressure. Policies of love were dictated by success, and failures were not merely stumbling blocks but weighty anchors pulling down the spirits of those who dared to miss the mark. The conflicting impressions of how father figures shaped lives sat heavy with Alex, aching like a reminder of expectations yet to be fulfilled.

As the ball rolled into the corner, Sam let out a squeal of delight at its newfound destination, clapping tiny hands together in a fleeting exchange of joy. Alex knelt beside his son, his heart swelling at the innocent expression of exuberance. Watching Sam revel in this simple exploration, he couldn't help but emulate the warmth he once received from his own dad. There was no room for strictness in the laughter of a child.

But as the day wore on, cracks began to emerge in Alex's idyllic vision of parenthood. Just as he sought to blend patience and encouragement, reality insisted on asserting itself, hurling obstacles in his direction. A concoction of sleep deprivation and the frenetic energy of a growing toddler seeped into the corners of his frazzled brain.

Sam launched himself off the living room couch for what Alex thought was an innocent leap, but laughter quickly spiraled into nervousness when the little one stumbled, tumbling headfirst onto a pile of cushions Alex had hastily arranged moments earlier. The muted thud echoed through the room, punctuated by a startled squeal that jerked Alex's heart into his throat.

Just like that, chaos reignited, sending Alex into a whirlwind of instincts: He darted towards Sam, a flurry of limbs and panic. In that split second, the ferocity of protective fatherhood surged through him, tethered to memories of what strictness might dictate—an echo of discipline that would chide Sam for being careless. But those thoughts collided with the vision of his own father, who always extended a hand of comfort rather than condemnation.

"Hey! It's alright, buddy, you're alright!" Alex crouched, wrapping his arms around Sam, pulling him close, his heart racing. The toddler blinked back tears and then burst into joyful giggles, bouncing against Alex's chest as if testing the very fabric of resilience.

In that moment, Alex remembered how his own father would crouch beside him after a fall or a misstep. Not as an executioner but as an anchor grounding him to the reassuring knowledge of unconditional love. His heart soared, knowing that despite the chaos around him, it was these tender moments that defined fatherhood, not the rigidness that had trapped his friend in a world of pressure.

The tidal wave of emotions danced through Alex, reminding him that every tumble and fall was merely a step in a long journey of discovery. As he held Sam close, a lump formed in his throat, realizing the emotional vulnerability he never wanted to suppress. Just as he had once found solace in his father's arms, he wanted Sam to know that he was cherished, no matter how many times he stumbled.

Days turned into weeks, and as the months passed, the life Alex was building began to feel like a mosaic—an eclectic gathering of nurturing warmth and moments wrought with uncertainty. Each family dinner was a cacophony of delightful chaos, with Sam finding new ways to explore vegetables, leading to a battle of wills over broccoli that replaced the serenity of the dining table with melodramatic performances. Each bite was met with comical disdain, and each moment of meal prep found Alex recalling his own father's patience, picturing the dance of coaxing and encouraging that had once taken place in their kitchen.

"Just try one little piece, buddy. It's good for you, I promise!" Alex played along, mimicking the gentle persuasion his dad often employed, reminding himself that sometimes a nurturing voice was all it took to make a child feel encouraged rather than forced.

Naturally, there were also nights of sheer pandemonium when Sam demanded to explore the depths of his imagination—specifically around 2 AM. One such infamous night, Alex found himself in the midst of an uproar at bedtime. Rocks of sleep clung to his eyes like cobwebs as Sam aimed his stuffed lion at the wall, remaking the living room into a battlefield where tigers roared and heroes were made in his imagination. Alex tried to keep the peace, yearning to quell the wildness of a child's spirit, but that desire often felt like an anchor weighing him down.

A sense of guilt washed over him, akin to the feel of his friend's father's rigid expectations flooding back to his mind. He envisioned those quiet dinners spent under the solemn gaze of strict discipline. Yet, in those sleepless nights, he recognized an irreplaceable truth: nurturing one's child was not without its chaos. It consisted of letting go of perfection and embracing the vibrant energy of imagination at its most raw.

When Sam finally collapsed into sleep, exhausted from all the fun and creativity, Alex found himself still awake. Sleepless nights turned into quiet moments for reflection; he felt torn between stitches from disparate worlds—caught between being the encouraging father his own dad had been and the strict, successful figure so ingrained in his social narrative.

On one hand, Alex aspired to replicate his father's tenderness. In between rounds of model-building and impromptu dance parties in the living room, he forged closer ties with Sam, diving into the heart of a relationship built on laughter and love. In the invisible tug-of-war between nurturing and rigid discipline, he was driven by a voice that urged him to foster connection over instruction.

On the other hand, parental anxiety often intruded, sprouting from moments of self-doubt—was he being too permissive? Would his son grow to appreciate discipline, something he had often associated with success? An inevitable cycle tugged at him mercilessly, forcing him to contemplate outcomes that were still too far down the road to grasp. He longed to embody the best of both worlds, creating a fatherly model where encouragement did not excuse laziness, and boundaries served to guide rather than stifle potential.

The physical environment also presented its own trials. Sam's burgeoning independence meant that Alex now found himself continually child-proofing the house in ways he had never imagined. What had once been a safe haven transformed into a landscape of hidden dangers—the edges of coffee tables, electrical outlets, and the staircase looming as an immense challenge.

Every corner of the house became a testament to rapid change. Each shelf was stripped bare of cherished memorabilia, replaced with an assortment of toys and bright books, and picture frames had to be relocated to avoid curious fingers. The scent of wood polish hung in the air as Alex hurried to secure the environment and safeguard his child, forced into the dual role of protector and provocateur.

As days turned into a blurred frenzy of chaotic laughter and moments of frustration, Alex discovered a peculiar beauty in the unpredictability of parenting. Schedules unraveled while a spirit of spontaneity unfolded. Every glowing smile on Sam's face lit up like fireworks, bringing warmth to the coldest, most stressful days. The joy carved out spaces for growth within him, urging him to revisit those fears of inadequacy that echoed from his friend and his friend's rigged approach.

The journey towards understanding fatherhood, he soon learned, would not follow neatly laid-out lines. In Sam's free spirit, Alex saw glimmers of himself—an echo of the boy he once was, unsure but hopeful. He smiled at the thought of how these raw moments would serve to shape not only his son's identity but also his own.

With each passing day, as Sam ventured forth into this exciting world of colors, sounds, and tastes, Alex found himself slowly redefining success. It wasn't about accolades or balance sheets; it was about forging connections and creating envisioning spaces for exploration where love reigned supreme. It was the laughter carried away on the wind, the gentle nudges, and the occasional bumps along the way that created the foundation for a strong and lasting bond.

By the end of the first year, Alex had unraveled the chaos enough to extract deep-seated meaning from the experience of fatherhood. The exhaustion and joy mingled into a kind of rhythm only they understood. Whenever he sat down beside Sam to build blocks or finger paint, he could feel the rhythms of laughter echoing in the background. The world outside may still demand its standards, but within their little patch of life, they were learning to explore and blossom together.

Alex realized he had long crossed the line from chaos into an extraordinary realm of consummate love, where nurturing reigns supreme over rigid expectations. He had not just survived the first year of parenthood; he had forged connections that would be needed to navigate this unpredictable journey ahead. Through this spiral of parental growth, he found solace, breathing life into the true essence of what it meant to be a good dad.

Lessons from Failure

In the soft, early light of dawn, as the first rays of sunshine crept through the sheer curtains of Alex's living room, he felt the familiar weight of the day ahead pressing down on him. There was a quiet chaos that enveloped the house, a subtle reminder of the responsibilities he had undertaken as a new father. With his son, Ethan, still nestled snugly in his crib, Alex took a moment to reflect on the challenges he faced as he attempted to create a semblance of routine in their lives.

The expectations had seemed so manageable before Ethan was born. Alex had envisioned cozy mornings filled with laughter, shared breakfasts, and intimate moments of bonding as they navigated through the realms of playtime and learning. However, the reality was vastly different. The idea of a scheduled routine felt like an elusive dream, slipping further away from his grasp as the days turned into a blur of feeding times, diaper changes, and desperate cries for attention.

The echoes of his father's teachings reverberated in his mind—the gentle nudges of advice seeped into his consciousness, urging him to seek a balanced approach to parenting. Yet, the lessons he had learned from his own father seemed to collide with the stern methods observed in his best friend's upbringing, leaving him perplexed and unsure how to forge his path.

As he prepared breakfast that morning, a cacophony of sounds filled the kitchen: the sizzling of bacon, the soft hum of water boiling for oatmeal, and Ethan's gurgling coos emanating from the next room. Alex felt a momentary rush of optimism as he pictured the day unfolding, hoping that today would be the day when everything fell into place—a day where the chaos harmoniously transformed into a flowing routine.

However, as the minutes dragged on, reality began to sink in. The tranquil morning was abruptly interrupted by a loud, discontented wail emanating from Ethan's crib. Instinctively, Alex's heart raced. Rushing to the nursery, he found Ethan's little face scrunched up in distress, fists balled at his sides, cries piercing through the air.

"Hey buddy, what's wrong?" Alex cooed, leaning down to lift Ethan into his arms. As he held his son, the warmth of the moment was overshadowed by a creeping anxiety.

Alex had always envisioned himself as a patient and nurturing father, but as he stood there, he could feel the impatience bubbling beneath the surface. Fleeting thoughts of his friend's father, with his strict disciplinary methods, flickered in his mind.

“Maybe I need to be a little tougher,” he muttered under his breath, trying to reconcile the contrasting influences on his parenting style. Yet each attempt to adopt discipline felt more like a patchwork response instead of a well-thought-out strategy. The realization that he was failing to establish a healthy routine weighed heavier with each waking moment.

After calming Ethan down with gentle kisses and sweet whispers, Alex set the toddler in his high chair for breakfast, determined to make the day work. But chaos quickly seeped back in.

Ethan seemed restless, flinging his drinks and food across the table as he squirmed in his seat, laughing at the dramatic mess he was creating. Alex’s initial thoughts of nurturing drifted into frustration, his attempt to maintain a semblance of order succumbing to the whirlwind of baby-led antics.

“Ethan, please don’t do that!” he raised his voice without realizing it, the sound startling his small son, whose laughter faded into confusion. The weight of guilt wrapped tightly around Alex’s heart. In that moment, the vision of the patient, loving father he wanted to be clashed brutally with his current state of overreaction and growing frustration.

As he transitioned from playfulness to disciplinary tactics, he found himself resorting to a half-hearted warning, hoping to regain control of the chaotic situation.

"Alright, if you keep throwing your food, we won't get to play with your favorite toys later."

Ethan let out a little wail. The redirection felt insufficient, the words hollow against the backdrop of a fragile moment. Alex could see the confusion in Ethan's eyes; the ethos of love and firmness was lost in translation. Their bond felt frayed.

After a few moments of ineffective discourse, Alex realized he was stepping into territory where discipline became a mask for his own fear of inadequacy. Here, as a father, he struggled to bring two polarized approaches together, aware now that every moment of failure led him toward an overwhelming feeling of guilt and self-doubt.

As Ethan continued to squirm and squeal, Alex finally reached his breaking point. Without thinking, he put his hands on the table and leaned toward his son, his face mere inches from Ethan's shocked expression.

"I said stop it!" he snapped, his voice harsh as he spoke the words before catching himself. He withdrew, stepping back as he watched the innocence in Ethan's eyes evaporate into a cloud of uncertainty.

It hadn't taken long, this unraveling, but the emotional fallout was instantaneous—Alex felt as if he had betrayed the very essence of the father he aspired to be.

In that disheartening moment, guilt washed over him like cold water. Alex's heart sank, recognizing that he had approached the situation with all the misguided rigidity he so despised. The iron hand in velvet gloves, the very source of his own fears, had crept into his methods. It had created a fracture completely counter to the loving embrace of his father.

The rest of the morning was a blur—a string of muted conversations that felt more like echoes of conflict rather than the tender exchanges he had hoped for. The mess from breakfast, with remnants of oatmeal and chunks of uneaten fruit strewn across the floor, felt like an accurate representation of his internal struggle. Everything had spiraled, and the weight of his misstep settled heavily on his shoulders, each breath tinged with the awareness that he could have handled it better.

Later that day, as Ethan napped peacefully in his crib, Alex leaned against the kitchen counter, hot mug of coffee gripped tightly in his hands. The room was still, but his mind was a whirlwind of thoughts—each a fragment of a parenthood that felt more daunting with every passing minute.

In an attempt to make sense of the morning, he reflected on his father's teachings—those moments filled with patience and understanding. Yet they felt so distant now, almost romanticized as he remembered the gentle nudges toward kindness and warmth. Alex could hear his father's voice in his head, reminding him that every child grows at their own pace, that each moment of chaos carries lessons waiting to unfold.

And here he was, chaotic routines spiraling out of control—a far cry from those idealized visions. A familiar frustration began to sneak back in, entangling itself with the guilt he felt. He longed to navigate the myriad of parenthood while emulating the values he was taught, yet how could he do that after failing at even the simplest task?

In that period of quiet self-reflection, Alex became acutely aware of the layers of failure he was confronting. It wasn't just about a messy breakfast or a reprimanded child; it went deeper, revealing the underlying question of what it truly meant to be a father—to find the balance between nurturing love and firm guidance. It made him realize that even the most loving fathers stumble, that every moment of discipline doesn't need to sound like a hammer falling, and that his emotional range was part of the journey.

With resolve, he sought a different approach, aware that he would need to actively work toward understanding rather than immediate reprimand.

As night fell, after Ethan had been tucked into bed, Alex found himself reflecting on the day. Although he had stumbled, the realization of what he had done wrong settled deep within him, prompting a need to reach out—to learn and to grow from this experience.

He picked up his phone, scrolling through messages, until he landed on a familiar name: Steven, his best friend. Although they had always shared different views on parenting, he knew that his friend's perspective might provide much-needed insight.

“Hey, can we talk?” he typed, almost hesitantly pressing send while second-guessing himself. Did he really want to share this feeling of vulnerability?

Soon after, a reply pinged back, leaving an outstretched hand offered in support. “Of course. Let's grab a drink tomorrow?”

As reality wound its way back, Alex could feel a flicker of hope—a renewed sense that he wasn't alone in this endeavor. That in sharing his mistakes, there could be growth. The shadows of failure began to lift, illuminating pathways through which clarity could be gained; he could find himself as a father still learning and still growing.

Thus, the journey of parenthood continued to unfold—a tapestry woven from successes and failures, each thread symbolizing the essential lessons gathered along the road. As Alex tucked away his reflections for the night, he found solace in knowing that even in moments of missteps, there always lay opportunities for redemption.

Tomorrow would be a new day, filled with challenges yet to come.

As sleep washed over him, Alex embraced the uncertainty that parenthood bore—a journey both beautiful and tumultuous, rich with lessons waiting to be learned.

Seeking Guidance

Alex sat on a weathered park bench, the sunlight filtering through the leaves overhead, casting intricate patterns on the ground below. All around him, children's laughter mingled with the sounds of parent-child interactions. It was a scene that should have felt idyllic, yet Alex felt an underlying tension threading through his chest. Today was one of those days when the weight of fatherhood pressed heavily upon him—the `why` of his decisions swirled in his mind alongside the `how` of managing his son's boundless energy.

He had decided to come to the park in hopes of finding more than just fresh air and a place to tire out his son—he was searching for guidance. The fear of failure loomed larger than ever, and his instinct was to reach out, to learn from those who walked similar paths of parenthood. As he scanned the playground, Alex noticed a small cluster of fathers gathered near the swings. They laughed, joked, and shared stories, their camaraderie evident. Though he often felt intimidated by their assuredness, a spark of determination ignited within him, compelling him to approach them.

"Hey, mind if I join?" he asked, willing his voice not to tremble. The group glanced over, and one father, a tall man with a scruffy beard and an easy smile, replied, "Of course! We could use more company."

As he settled down on the grass beside them, Alex felt an impending sense of relief wash over him—a sense that perhaps he could glean something valuable from their conversations. The father beside him introduced himself as Mike, a seasoned dad of three, whose love for hiking often spilled over into family adventures.

"So, what's your parenting philosophy? Are you more of a hands-on kind of dad or do you lean towards letting them figure things out?" Mike asked, his tone light yet genuinely curious.

Alex hesitated, masking bubbles of uncertainty that threatened to burst. "Uh, well, honestly, I'm still trying to figure that out. I grew up with a dad who was really nurturing, always encouraging me, and… my best friend had a dad who was all about discipline and tough love. Now, I'm just stuck trying to find a middle ground."

Mike nodded appreciatively. "I get that. It can feel like a maze trying to navigate everything. I remember being caught between wanting to be the fun dad and also teaching discipline."

The conversation unfolded, and soon other fathers chimed in with their own stories. Each new narrative painted a broader picture of the complexities and joys of fatherhood, each man echoing Alex's struggles in different tones.

"Let me tell you about a time I got it all wrong," interrupted Eric, a sharply dressed father with a friendly grin. "I planned this big bike trip for my son's birthday—it was going to be a day filled with laughter and adventure! But on the way, he fell off his bike and scraped his knee. I rushed over, but rather than comfort him, I inadvertently pushed him to get back up and keep going. It was all I'd learned about resilience in my own upbringing. But it backfired. He ended up crying, and I felt like a total failure."

Every heartbeat felt amplified in Alex's chest as he listened, nodding along. Eric's words struck a chord. It was all too familiar; the struggle to balance resilience with gentle guidance. "How did you handle it afterward?" Alex asked.

Eric smiled sheepishly. "Well, that evening, I apologized. I told him it was okay to feel upset, that sometimes falling down is part of the journey—and the following day, we took our bikes to the park just to enjoy the ride. No expectations, no pressure. I learned to let him express himself."

The vulnerability in Eric's confession validated Alex's own fears. He felt less isolated in his confusion and anxiety. Even the seemingly perfect fathers faced their own crises of confidence.

"Sounds like you found a way to balance discipline and compassion," Alex remarked, finding motivation in the encounter. He sensed warmth not only in their shared experiences but also in knowing it was okay to stumble.

As the group continued sharing stories, another father, Sam, chimed in with an outspoken voice full of conviction. “You know, my dad was strict. Taught me that love was shown through hard lessons—first, you fall. Then, you learn to get back up. But I’ve got three girls, and I’ve realized kindness is way more important than anything else.”

Alex perked up. The blend of sentiments—the realities of parenting lived through encouragement and firmness—were beginning to shape a tapestry of understanding.

“What works for you?” Alex asked.

Sam chuckled. “I try to meet them where they are. We talk through their feelings, often over ice cream! I want them to know they can trust me. Believing in them means the world.”

“That’s the goal, isn’t it?” Mike chimed back in, glancing at the other fathers before returning his gaze to Alex. “Our kids are learning from us whether we direct their paths or give them room to explore. I always remind my kids it’s okay to fail.”

Murmurs of agreement rolled through the small circle, filling the air with a collective understanding of this shared journey of parenthood. Each father’s narrative intertwined into an evolving lesson, offering varying ideologies sandwiched between empathy and experience—built on a foundation of vulnerability that felt oddly comforting.

As the sun began to meander lower in the sky, casting a warm golden hue over the park, Alex’s spirit lifted. Every story offered like a small gift sparked an expansion of his perspective. “Do you think there’s a middle pathway?” he ventured, feeling bolder now.

"Definitely. It's about trusting your instincts, adjusting as your kids grow, and being present," Mike replied firmly. "You'll mess up; we all have. But what matters is how you respond. There's no manual—the heart of fatherhood is about continuous adaptation."

Alex's mind raced with the encounters from that day. Each conversation had provided fragile insights, woven together in stark contrast to the rigid definitions he'd previously fought against. The universal feelings of doubt blended seamlessly with deep-rooted love. After hours of laughter and camaraderie, Alex realized he wasn't looking for a definitive answer but rather the understanding that parenting amounted to malleable practices and choices made daily.

Feeling armed with newfound insights, Alex watched the children dash about, carefree and wild. His son, tumbling into a patch of grass, erupted into joyful giggles. The image tugged at his heart, igniting the warmth of possibility within. Colliding emotions pressed upon him—excitement, confusion, and the most comforting of all: community.

He bid farewell to the fathers that day, their stories etched into a corner of his mind. As he packed their snacks and hoisted his son onto his hip, Alex sensed a shift circulating within. He had stepped out of his isolated thoughts and embraced the experiences of a collective fatherhood that rang with perpetual learning.

Each of those encounters would echo, compelling him to be brave enough to blend his father's encouragement with the lessons learned from his friend's tough love. Alex returned home with a detailed story freshly painted, a mosaic of insights that created an evolving approach to fatherhood.

In the weeks that followed, he found himself gravitating back toward the park, drawn by the magnetic hope that community provided. Each meeting unfolded more lessons, each father representing a thread in the tapestry of experience he sought to weave. And soon enough, the casual chat at the swings transformed into emotional discussions of parenthood—spurring insights rich with vulnerability and honesty.

One afternoon, he sat at a picnic table beside a father named Tom, a laid-back guy with a penchant for dad jokes. Tom's easygoing demeanor masked the profound reflections stirred within his stories, which occurred mostly during lawn-mowing mishaps or backyard barbecue disasters.

"I was out there trying to show my son how to grill burgers, right?" Tom chuckled, wiping a hand across his forehead. "And the first ones? Burnt. I was mortified. My son looked at me like I'd lost all sense of authority!"

Alex echoed the laughter but took notice of Tom's shifting tones. "What changed?" he asked, genuinely curious.

Tom sighed happily, "Instead of hiding it, I leaned into it. I said, 'Well, buddy, looks like we've learned our first lesson today: how not to grill burgers!' And then together we figured it out, laughing through the mistakes."

"Embracing the failures," Alex murmured. The realization hit home; he was often terrified of being wrong. Perhaps those little moments provided the best lessons—the most human glimpses into fatherhood.

"Exactly," Tom replied, grinning widely. "It's vulnerability. Being real with them—putting down perfection for connection."

The park continued to thrive around them; children shouted with joy, not faltering in their quest to dominate the monkey bars, and their parents, like Alex, observed, shared, and reflected. He felt among a kinship that softened the jagged edges within him—one that understood the duality of fatherhood and the impact of each interaction.

Later that week, Alex found himself in an art class for parents at the community center. The instructor, a friendly woman named Maya, held a vibrant personality that lit up the small classroom. "Today's project involves creating a collage that represents our journey as parents," she declared. "Feel free to use anything that speaks to you—images, words, colors!"

As Alex dug through the supplies, something ignited his creativity, leading him to formulate an image that encapsulated both his upbringing and the stories shared among the fathers he had met. He pieced together a representation—a half-light, half-dark silhouette; the light cascaded over nurturing lines, while shadows danced into the frame, delineating moments of tougher love learned from his best friend's experience.

Maya strolled around, observing the burgeoning collages and pausing by Alex's piece. "I see a blend here," she noted. "A beautiful balance of softness and strength. It's powerful. Why did you choose this visual representation?"

He paused, weighing the interdependence within—"It felt raw. I'm trying to find that blend of nurturing, like my dad, with the strength of setting boundaries. It's about how I believe I can help my son grow into the person he needs to be."

"That's poignant, Alex," she replied, taking a step back to admire the creativity. "There's so much depth in what you've shared. This is precisely how parenting works—it's about finding that balance in our unique ways."

As each father's journey unfurled into their own worlds, Alex found beauty in the simplicity of connecting, a space where they could talk about everything from parenting blunders to moments of triumph. A mutual understanding blossomed in their conversations, a network of support that began to soften the entrapments of self-doubt as he embraced their diverse experiences.

Days turned into weeks, and Alex's.son thrived in this new environment—each day marked with laughter and the inevitable challenges that shaped their days together. His courage in seeking guidance began to turn the wheels of confidence within him, and as he learned, he could forgive both himself and the misconceptions he had harbored about fatherhood.

In every story exchanged at the park, from the laughter shared around the grill to the vivid colors of the art class, Alex developed a profound understanding: parenting is not merely about choosing right from wrong; it emanates from connection, love, and a communal narrative that weaves through their shared journey.

And with that realization, he left the park, heart full and anchored with hope, stepping confidently toward a fatherhood defined not by the weight of expectations but rather by the joy of adventure and learning. In connecting with others, he found the path to clarity and a deeper understanding—his journey would forever be enhanced by the laughter and lessons shared with those around him.

In that moment of stepping away from self-inflicted isolation, toward a space of shared experience, Alex understood what it meant to embrace fatherhood fully. Rather than battling the shadows of comparison, he was weaving a beautiful tapestry that encompassed both gentleness and strength, illuminated by the stories of fathers who had walked beside him in their shared odyssey.

Lessons from the Playground

The Melting Pot of Stories

The sun hung high in the sky, casting a gentle warmth over the playground, where the laughter of children fused with the sounds of squeaking swings and the rhythmic thud of small feet running on gravel. The air was thick with the smell of freshly cut grass, mingling with the enticing aroma of nearby food trucks offering hot dogs and cotton candy. It was a haven—a vibrant tapestry of colors and sounds, where innocence thrived and community blossomed amongst those who gathered.

Alex stood near the edge of the playground, leaning against the splintered wood of the old fence, a soft smile playing across his lips as he observed the scene before him. His son, a tiny whirlwind of energy, darted from the sandbox to the swing set, his laughter ringing like a sweet melody. Each time the little boy pushed himself higher, swinging into the air with unabashed delight, Alex felt a surge of warmth in his chest. Here, amidst the chaos, was a sense of freedom and joy that brought back flickers of his own childhood.

He spotted a group of fathers clustered together, their animated discussions blending into a symphony of voices that filled the air. Each of them had a child or two engaging in the various activities of the playground, from climbing the jungle gym to chasing after a rogue soccer ball. The fathers, diverse in background and appearance, stood united by the common thread of parenthood.

One father, sporting a navy blue baseball cap turned backward, animatedly recounted a camping trip gone awry. He gestured wildly, illustrating how his son had mistakenly set off their portable grill. "I swear, it looked like a scene from a movie! Flames, smoke, and my kid just staring at it, wide-eyed!" The other fathers erupted into laughter, their easy camaraderie evident.

Beside him stood a dad with a beaming smile, nodding in sympathy. "I remember when my daughter tried to roast marshmallows over a bonfire with a stick she thought was a sword. Let's just say, she might be a knight in her imagination, but that day ended with a roasted marshmallow disaster!" A chuckle spread among the group, and Alex felt warmth radiate from their easy friendship, a bond woven through shared experiences and the chaos of parenting.

As he watched, Alex couldn't help but feel a twinge of admiration. These fathers traded stories like precious heirlooms, each tale a testament to the trials of fatherhood, the moments of glory, the mishaps, and the lessons learned amid the laughter. For each father, their children's milestones echoed their efforts as parents, infusing strength into their identities.

Alex approached, drawn into the soft orbit of their laughter. "Mind if I join?" he asked, a genuine smile brightening his face. The group welcomed him warmly, making space for his presence, their stories momentarily paused in favor of his arrival.

"We were just sharing war stories about our latest adventures with the kids," the cap-wearing dad explained, inviting Alex into the fold. "You got any tales to share?"

Alex chuckled, his heart racing slightly at the prospect of sharing. Each story he recounted became more than just recollections; they morphed into lessons that elucidated the essence of fatherhood, guiding lights on his journey.

"Well," he began, taking a deep breath, "the other day, my son had his first encounter with a bee. There we were, enjoying a picnic in the backyard, and all of a sudden, he spotted the little creature buzzing near the sandwich. You could see fear flash across his face—'Daddy, is it going to sting me?' And I thought for a second, should I be calm and nurturing, or should I teach him to be brave and face his fears? So, I opted for both. I said, 'You're safe! Let's just watch it. Bees are our friends, after all!' That turned into a whole twenty-minute lesson on how bees help flowers and why they're important. Nothing like a bee to spark a life lesson!"

Laughter erupted again. The fathers leaned in closer, reflecting their understanding and appreciation of the struggles inherent in balancing nurturing and teaching. In that moment, Alex realized that vulnerability was a currency in this community of fathers, and sharing tales of triumph and trials became a thread binding them together.

As the conversations flowed, more stories surfaced. The dad with the knight's sword recalled how his daughter had also developed a fascination with imaginary foes during their last park visit, where her vivid imagination turned the jungle gym into a dragon's lair. "I ended up being the villain in her story! I thought my role was to chase away playtime thieves, but in her eyes, I was the dragon! That play fight lasted an hour. My goodness, the stamina those little ones have!"

The laughter was infectious, and Alex found himself reminiscing about creative moments with his son, who could transform the simplest objects—a cardboard box—into a spaceship. With infectious glee, Alex shared, "Not just a spaceship, but a galaxy far, far away! He insisted I wear a helmet made of tinfoil! And when we blasted off, it was like nothing else existed."

The interplay of joyous laughter and heartfelt connections painted a vivid picture of their lives; Alex realized he was not alone in navigating the confusing waters of fatherhood. Each father shared not just stories, but emotions; fears mingled with hope, triumphs sprouted from struggles. The playground became a sanctuary where vulnerability was welcomed—a melting pot of shared experiences soaking into the soil of friendship.

As the sunset painted the skies in hues of orange and pink, the conversations turned more reflective. One father, a tall man with a gentle demeanor, spoke up about parental worries, his voice dipping slightly. "You know, despite all the fun, sometimes it gets heavy. I worry about my son's future—school, friends, making the right choices. It's overwhelming, isn't it? Every day, I wonder if I'm doing enough."

Nods of understanding rippled through the group, acknowledgment of the weight they all carried as guiding fathers. Alex could see reflections of his own thoughts mirrored in their expressions.

"It's like we learn as we go," said Alex, interjecting. "Every mistake feels monumental at the moment, but these moments we share—frustration, joy—they're the threads that weave the fabric of our parenting. I think as long as we show up, we're doing something right."

The father with the blue cap shared, "Absolutely! These stories help me remember the joy and laughter in the chaos, remind me that I'm not alone in feeling like I'm winging it most of the time. Even when I feel like I'm not enough, moments like these ground me."

Their camaraderie deepened, weaving each father into a supportive network, where doubt could transform into encouragement, where fear could blossom into courage. As more stories flowed, Alex reflected on how these shared moments brought forth insights that would influence his approach to fatherhood. Each tale became a touchstone, guiding him through uncertainty, illuminating his path.

Other fathers chimed in with their own tales of reflection, poignant musings sprinkled with humor about their own fathers, the legacy of generational parenting styles intermingling with their hopes for their children.

One father, whose son had taken to climbing every conceivable surface with the zest of a mountain goat, explained, "There's a fine line between encouraging independence and worrying they might fall. I constantly battle with that hesitation! But every step they take toward independence means they're growing. Honestly, I might be more scared than my son each time he veers off a ledge!"

Their laughter was deeper now, born from shared recognition of hovering fears that intertwined with unwavering devotion. In a world where expectations loomed large, they found solace in their vulnerabilities, where each laughed worry was a testament to their shared journey.

As dusk began to settle, the playground transformed into a magical realm where shadows danced against the fading light. The children's laughter became a distant echo, creating a backdrop for the men to navigate deeper into more profound discussions. They painted vivid pictures of their aspirations and dreams for their children—the kind of futures they sought to build despite their own insecurities.

"I just hope my son grows up kind, thoughtful, and brave—all those qualities I sometimes question in myself," the gentle-faced father mused, his voice softening. "But isn't that what we strive for? To mirror the best parts of ourselves back to them?"

There was a collective nod as agreements seeped into the air like warmth from an embrace. With each shared insight, Alex felt a connection solidifying the fabric of friendship, unity forged through recognizing how they battled similar internal struggles.

Finally, as the sun dipped below the horizon, obscuring the playground in shades of twilight, Alex caught sight of his son, exhilarated, leaping off the swing like a wild bird breaking free from its nest. The moment encapsulated the essence of childhood—fearlessly chasing after unattainable dreams, undeterred by fallibility.

Alex turned back to his newfound friends, a content smile crossing his face. "You know what? Watching him play like that reminds me of how resilient they are. It makes me reflect on how important it is to just step back and let them fly."

The heartfelt understanding encircled them like a warm embrace; they exchanged knowing glances, words commingling in heartfelt acknowledgment. Alex realized that while their playground stories were steeped in humor and warmth, beneath each anecdote existed a shared philosophy, a deep understanding that, ultimately, they were all navigating the beautiful chaos together.

As they carried their conversations deeper into the evening, the fathers had unwittingly gathered a treasure trove of stories—simple snippets infused with wisdom and hope. They were a collection of lessons, emblematic of the unbreakable bonds that tie fathers to their children, reflecting the joys and trials; they were a melting pot of tales blending laughter and tears, cementing the core of their journeys.

With the stars beginning to twinkle overhead and the universe settling into a quiet night, Alex felt grateful—grateful for the serendipitous moments of validation, for the openness of the fathers around him, and the laughter that echoed like a soothing balm as they all embraced the adventure before them.

As the evening drew to a close, they exchanged smiles and goodbyes filled with unspoken promises—each silently pledging to cherish these moments and continue sharing their stories. In this sanctuary of the playground—this melting pot of experiences—they had forged not just friendships but a community, reaffirming the undeniable truth that parenting, with all its intricacies, was a journey best taken together.

Contrasting Values

The sunny afternoon was alive with the laughter of children darting across the playground, a cacophony of joy that enveloped Alex as he stood by the swings. The golden rays filtered through the green leaves above, casting playful shadows over the well-worn woodchips. It was an arena of discovery where children climbed, toppled, and emerged triumphantly from their mini adventures, and for Alex, it was also a place of revelation. Here, amid the jubilant cries and the rhythmic squeak of the swings, he would encounter a spectrum of fatherhood, each offering lessons that sharpened his understanding of what it meant to be a dad.

As he pushed his son Tyler on the swing, he observed the thrumming life around him. To his left was Mark, a fellow dad known for his laid-back parenting style. Mark crafted an image of a father who favored an approach that was almost Zen-like in its tranquility. Family outings often saw him leaning back in a folding chair, beer in hand, as his kids rummaged through the adjacent sandpit without a single care. Underneath this calm exterior, Alex sensed an undercurrent of nonchalance in Mark's parenting.

"Hey, Alex! You ought to let Tyler explore more," Mark called out, his carefree grin illuminated by the sun. "Kids need to find their own way, you know? We can’t always swoop in to save them. They learn from their mistakes!"

Alex chuckled, feeling the familiar tug between admiration for Mark's conviction and a trace of doubt. Was it viable, this idea that parenting could hinge on an absence of intervention? As Tyler soared higher with each push, Alex saw his son's little legs kick against the air with pure glee, and yet he also couldn't ignore the fleeting moments when Tyler would almost topple and need guidance to steady himself. What if he didn't realize he needed help?

Nearby sat Robert, a steadfast traditionalist who defined fatherhood in resolute, time-tested terms. With his neatly combed hair and crisp collared shirt, Robert controlled the scene with an air of authority that echoed his childhood experiences. He often dropped references about how discipline had shaped the great men of history. "Respect and obedience are crucial," Robert would often argue with an almost academic slant. "If children don't learn this early, how will they function in the world?"

Sitting on a bench with his arms crossed, he turned his stern gaze toward his own children, who were engaged in a fierce game of tag. "Boys, focus on the goal! Don't just run around aimlessly!" he barked, sending a ripple of tension into the playful atmosphere.

Alex observed the children's reactions—immediate compliance, yet a tangible shadow over their laughter. It was evident that Robert's children respected him, but at what cost? As they snapped to attention with goosebumps raised from his authority, Alex frowned in reflection. Could such rigidity foster true joy, or would it merely impose an artificial structure that stripped away their natural exuberance?

Amidst these competing paradigms, Alex felt a growing discomfort—a realization that he was standing at a crossroads. As he watched Tyler's blissful yet occasionally tumultuous swing experience, he pondered his own parenting style. Deep down, he craved the warmth and emotional understanding his father had imparted through gentleness and love. But how did he appease the subtle murmurs of doubt that floated around him, like leaves in the gentle breeze?

Just then, Mark ambled over with a knowing smirk. "You look troubled, my friend. Caught between a rock and a hard place?" He nudged Alex in a friendly manner, his demeanor as relaxed as ever.

"It's just... I see how you let your kids wander free, and then there's Robert, all strict and orderly. It makes me wonder which end of the spectrum to lean toward. I mean, what do you think it means to be a good father?" Alex's voice held a thread of uncertainty, each word hanging in the sunlight.

Mark leaned back, the corners of his mouth twitching into a slight smile. "Being a good father means being available, Alex. Let them explore. Let them make their own decisions, even if they scrape their knees a bit. That's how they grow."

Alex considered this perspective, turning to watch Tyler yelling and jumping in the sand, seconds away from potential disaster as he stumbled on a mound. Impulsively, Alex started to step forward but hesitated. Was Mark right? Were those scrapes a necessity?

It was then that Robert joined their conversation. "Explore? Sounds like a recipe for disaster. Children need structure. I believe in teaching my kids from day one about the world's rules." Robert clasped his hands on his knees, appearing every bit the wise educator. "Discipline teaches them respect and keeps them safe. You can't let them run wild without guidance."

The exchange hung heavy in the air, like a clashing thunder of ideologies ready to burst. Alex felt the pull of both worlds. He admired Mark's approach—the carefree laughter that accompanied his children as they played. But he also recognized the tangible success stories in Robert's children. Their disciplined nature, while tinged with pressure, bore fruit in the form of awards and achievements.

The discussion unfolded other layers of their beliefs as they shared more tales, punctuating their exchanges with laughter as well as moments of solemnity. Mark, recalling an adventurous hiking trip where his children slipped and fell but ultimately navigated through under his watchful eye, added, "They've learned resilience! Think about it, that's crucial for later in life!"

Conversely, Robert recounted strict mornings filled with routine practice, discipline carved into each day like granite. "My son just took home a gold medal from his last competition! That's evidence of hard work from strict guidance, my friends." The pride in his voice was undeniable.

Alex leaned in, intrigued, but also enveloped by unease—a ping-pong match between competing philosophies that mirrored his internal conflicts. Could he genuinely hammer out a course that married the warmth of affection with the assertiveness of discipline?

As lively discussions continued around him, Alex engaged in his thoughts, reflecting on childhood lessons imbued with warmth. Echoes of his own father's nurturing ways made him consider how essential emotional connection was, helping to bridge the gap between discipline and freedom. Each story surrounding him sculpted his understanding of fatherhood into a varied masterpiece, and yet each layer of discussion revealed the fractures—the midpoints where children found themselves molded by conflicting ideals.

The more he listened, the more he realized how synthesized parenting models could be, weaving together threads of understanding while accepting the messiness of childhood and its inherent lessons.

“Look,” Mark interjected, catching Alex’s eye, “there’s no perfect way to parent. Sometimes you just have to let go. Let them feel slightly out of control so they can learn where the boundaries lie.”

Robert shook his head but didn’t dismiss the idea outright. “Letting them run free can only go so far. I’ve seen kids act up because there were no guidelines. They need to know consequences.” He wore the countenance of a man with a cause, and it sparked an idea in Alex’s mind—balance.

Suddenly Tyler called out from the swings, the sound of his voice slicing through the heated exchange. “Daddy! Watch me!”

As the little boy interpreted the situation, Alex immediately pivoted, abandoning their conversation to witness the moment. Tyler pumped his legs harder, pushing himself skyward as if attempting to break the horizontal terrain of the world. There was no doubt—his son was lost in the moment, a young airliner reaching for heights unknown.

But as Alex stood there, absorbed in his son's joy, a realization dawned on him: maybe the answers existed not in singular philosophies absolved of contradiction but rather in their intersection—the convergence of nurturing bonds and understanding boundaries. Each father brought lessons that resonated, threads that, when combined, wove together a device for effective parenting.

“Can we just meet halfway?” Alex queried, breaking through the tension like a warm sunbeam after a storm.

Both Mark and Robert paused, exchanging glances that revealed what had previously seemed unyielding. Slowly, they smiled at each other, even as Alex elucidated the essence of his request. “What if we took bits from both approaches? What if we let our kids explore just a little, but with some clear distinctions?”

Mark nodded, receptiveness glimmering in his eyes. “That’s interesting, man. Kids flourish best when given some license, but that doesn’t count out your side either. Perhaps structure is a necessary tool.”

Robert scratched his chin, his frown melting into contemplation. “And a degree of freedom might lend our children the opportunity to discover for themselves. But the principles remain vital.” He appeared as if he were unraveling a complex puzzle, knitting together doctrines once held fiercely apart.

“Precisely,” Alex confirmed, feeling a warmth spread within him. “Imagine the strength they'd have if they could learn respect while also feeling unencumbered.”

The playground around them seemed to swell with laughter, each curl of joy enveloping their discussions as they found common ground. The children executed a magical dance, exploring without the weight of parental pressure while absorbing small lessons of independence.

In that moment, the vibrant tapestry that had felt disjointed earlier began to stitch itself into something cohesive, replete with the contrasting values that each father offered. It was a brilliant amalgam—one that accepted complexities yet held space for kids to grow through their experiences, lessons learned, and mistakes made.

As the sun dipped lower in the sky, casting long shadows across the playground, Alex could feel a change taking hold. An invaluable lesson turned within—the kind that enveloped his heart and mind, merging ideals into a unique parenting adventure underpinned by love.

With newfound resolve, he couldn't wait to experiment with this meld of values at home. The playground had become a melting pot of discovery, and as he turned to watch Tyler soar higher on the swing, Alex marveled at the merging of elements. In the enchanting chaos of fatherhood, there lay potential—an opportunity to craft boundless lessons emerging from a loving embrace of contrasts, nurtured through a blend of skills and perspectives that ultimately shaped the way choices were made.

That afternoon, a promise was etched in his heart: the lessons learned would echo, not just for himself but for all his friends as they ventured through the landscapes of their own parenting journeys. With every choice they made, there lay a testament to the beauty of blending diverse values—a path toward the light, shining bright through the embrace of understanding.

Sharing Vulnerabilities

As the sun dipped lower on the horizon, casting long, playful shadows across the playground, Alex felt a sense of camaraderie envelop him. The shrieks of laughter from children echoed around him, punctuated by the soft whispers of fathers sharing stories on nearby benches. It was a lively scene, ripe with the gleeful chaos of children chasing one another, their boundless energy transforming the simple playground into a vibrant tapestry of life.

Alex shifted on the wooden bench, his thoughts drifting from the joyous chaos to the men around him. Each father had their own style of parenting visible through the way they interacted with their children. While one father sat with a soft smile, gently encouraging his daughter to try climbing to the highest rung of the jungle gym, another stood firmly at the base with crossed arms, watching his son take risks that pushed the boundaries of safety. The air was thick with the heady aroma of freshly mowed grass and the laughter of children, yet underneath, a current of tension existed—a palpable reminder of the doubts that lurked within each of the men present.

It was during these moments of watching the fathers interact that Alex began to notice subtle vulnerabilities peeking through their confident façades. Sure, the tales they exchanged seemed lighthearted on the surface, brimming with playful competition over who had the worst night without sleep or who had mastered the intricacies of diaper changes. Still, there were moments when their bravado cracked, revealing a more profound connection woven from shared experiences and the burdens they carried.

One evening, as the air began to cool and the golden light transformed into a softer hue, a father named Mark, who had earlier appeared stoic, looked over at Alex with a sigh that spoke volumes. He ran a hand through his hair and said, "You know, I thought I knew what to expect with my son, but sometimes I feel completely lost." The admission hung in the air, drawing Alex's attention from the playground antics as he turned toward Mark with curiosity.

"I get that," Alex replied, feeling a wave of empathy wash over him. "There are days I wonder if I'm doing anything right at all." The honesty that slipped out surprised even him. It was a moment where vulnerability became a bridge rather than a barrier, and from that point, something shifted among the fathers.

Mark leaned in closer, his voice low as if sharing a secret. "I worry I'm pushing him too hard. I want him to succeed, to be better than I was, but what if I'm pushing him away instead?"

Alex could feel the weight of Mark's words clinging in the air like fog. It mirrored a sentiment that he had wrestled with since becoming a father himself—was he nurturing his son's dreams or stifling them with his expectations? The ever-present question hung between the two men as they bonded over their shared realization that fatherhood was an intricate dance of love and fear.

As Alex absorbed those words, he began to listen more closely to the conversations happening around him. Each father, in their own way, expressed a deep sense of concern for their children. There was Ted, who proudly recounted a recent achievement of his son only to follow it up with the admission that every victory came with sleepless nights and second-guessing every decision he made along the way. Ted's laugh was tinged with sadness, and Alex realized that behind the humor lay a parent desperately navigating the rough waters of self-doubt.

The interactions amongst the fathers became an orchestra of emotions; there was laughter that rang through the air, yes, but beneath it was a profound honesty. They spoke of their struggles, insecurities, and aspirations for their children amid all the joyful noise. Each confession seemed to resonate with someone else in the group, sparking a ripple of shared understanding.

On another occasion, while watching the small bodies climb and tumble, Alex found himself sitting beside Nate. Between sips of lukewarm coffee, Nate divulged a different kind of struggle. “I'm not really there for my daughter, you know? I work long hours, and I feel like I’m missing so much. I keep telling myself it’s for her future, but I can see the disappointment in her eyes.” His voice cracked slightly, revealing the soul of a father caught between ambition and presence.

“I know what you mean,” Alex responded softly. “Sometimes, I feel like I’m physically present but mentally miles away.” The words poured out, bursting forth with surprising urgency. Here, amid the chaos of children at play, Alex found space to reconsider the values he held dear.

Nate looked at him, recognition dawning. “Yeah! It’s hard to strike that balance. We think we’re doing right by them, but what if they need us just to be there?” In that moment, Alex recognized a kinship not grounded solely in fatherhood but rooted in the shared reality of imperfect existence.

As the evenings went by and the playground became their meeting place, Alex felt the walls around his heart begin to soften. The conversations shared with the other fathers unearthed a raw vulnerability within him. He recalled the pressures surrounding his own upbringing—the desire to be like his nurturing father, to embody the wisdom and warmth he had received while trying to avoid the coldness of strict expectation.

One evening stood out distinctly: the fathers had gathered particularly late, when the sun had dipped below the horizon, and the streetlamps flickered on, bathing the playground in a warm glow. They sat scattered across the benches, recalling their childhood memories, when Ted suddenly asked, "What did your fathers teach you that you're afraid of replicating?"

After a moment of contemplative silence, Alex spoke up. "My father was soft, you know? He taught me about kindness and patience, but sometimes I wonder if that made me soft too. I want to instill strength in my son, but I fear inadvertently doing the opposite." The fear of failing his child began to ring true, as if it echoed the very fears shared by the others.

"I get that," Mark chimed in. "My dad was tough; he believed in discipline. But as much as I admired his strength, I often felt disconnected from him—like I was achieving everything for him and not for myself. I want to avoid that." The chorus of agreement was palpable, resonating within the collective consciousness of the group.

That night, vulnerability carved paths into deeper conversations, unlocking a space filled with empathy and understanding. They weren't just fathers knee-deep in the parenting trenches; they were men grappling with fears, desires, and the haunting specters of their own childhoods shaping their decisions.

Alex began to recognize how important these shared vulnerabilities were, how they allowed him to dissect his expectations of fatherhood and reflect on what truly mattered—love, connection, and understanding as the bedrock of parenthood rather than rigid discipline or ruthless ambition.

The more he shared, the less lonely he felt. As conversations persisted, Alex could sense the level of camaraderie deepen. Each father's stories painted a picture—not just of their aspirations but also their frustrations, their light and shadow intermingled; the symbols of what made them human. It was liberating, tearing down the constructed ideologies that had dictated their existence.

The playground transformed into a sanctuary of sorts, where they could gloat about their children's tiny milestones while tethering themselves with raw and unfiltered emotions swelling beneath surface-level pleasantries. As weeks melted into months, they began inviting their vulnerabilities into discussions more freely—a sense of liberation that came from sharing insecurity. The banter shifted; it became a tapestry woven with vulnerability and strength.

One afternoon, as they watched their children play, a moment of stillness descended over the group. The laughter of children melted into the background as each father confronted a moment of honesty. "What if we're the very threat we fear?" as one father posed. "What if we're more like our fathers than we want to admit?" His voice trembled, casting the group in thoughtful silence.

Alex felt a swirl of emotions; guilt, fear, and frustration danced within him. He reflected on the ways he often found himself mirroring his father, and like tendrils of smoke, memories of his own upbringing surfaced. That was what made the exchanges so profound—moments like these were transformative, prompting deeper thought and igniting sparks of grit and growth through shared wisdom.

"Maybe it's not about choosing one side or another," Nate mused, breaking the silence. "Maybe we just have to embrace both. Nurture alongside discipline." The quiet understanding amongst the group assured him he wasn't alone. Slowly, Alex felt the scaffolding of his own fatherly narrative tightening around him, firmly grasped by threads of balance amid the tug of expectation.

The balance they strove for was not a prescribed formula but a symphony—a delicate harmony of notes played with victims of their experiences, fragile but immensely beautiful. They breathed life into an understanding that being a father is filled with uncertainty and fluidity, blooming alongside the eagerness of their children.

Through shared vulnerability, they unearthed an unintentional power: the recognition that it is perfectly fine to be less than perfect. As they laughed and cried together, rhythmically exchanged stories of personal failures and victories alike, a bond and support forged around their insecurities began to shine brighter than the playground lights.

As the last whisps of light faded from the sky, Alex made a silent vow to carry forward the lessons learned among this band of fathers—each wrestling with their demons, each bearing the weight of their fears yet standing strong together against the trials of parenthood. In this community of shared vulnerability, he found not only understanding but a new belief in the beauty of imperfection in fatherhood.

Alex watched as his son, unaware of the struggles looming over his father's heart, laughed and played without a care in the world. It struck him then—the beautiful dichotomy of existence. While fragility marked their journey as fathers, the laughter of their children served as a reminder of hope, love, and the potential that every day unfolded.

In the end, it was the acknowledgment of their flaws, their raw expressions of vulnerabilities, that bound them together. These moments paved the way for deeper connections, allowing them all to reassess their beliefs about parenting. The playground, with its joyous chaos of life, became a canvas for growth—a place where they could both confront and celebrate the complexities of fatherhood together.

The War of the Roses

Confrontation at Home

The evening light filtered through the kitchen window, casting warm hues on the worn farmhouse table around which the family gathered for dinner. It should have been a peaceful scene, a moment of shared laughter and warmth. Instead, the room felt heavy with unspoken tension, the air thick with anticipation. Alex and his wife, Sarah, sat opposite each other, their plates untouched as an unvoiced dispute simmered just beneath the surface.

Alex's brow furrowed as he listened to his son's excited tales of the day, the way the little boy's eyes lit up when discussing his latest playground adventures. In those moments, Alex felt the profound joy of being a father. But it was that same joy that quickly twisted into an undercurrent of frustration as he remembered the conversation that had triggered this evening's contention.

"I don't see why you can't just let him be, Alex. He's five! He needs to explore and play, not be micromanaged every moment of his life." Sarah's voice was tinged with exasperation, each word sharp against the soft illumination of the setting sun.

Alex clenched his jaw, feeling his defenses rising like a fortress around his heart. "And what if he gets hurt? What if he doesn't learn discipline? He needs structure!" It was a classic argument, one that had graced their lips before, yet here they were again, standing in opposition to each other in a fearful dance of parenting philosophies.

In Alex's mind, he could hear the echoes of his father's words, the gentle reminders of empathy and kindness, juxtaposed with the rigid lessons learned from his friend's father, a man who wielded discipline like a hammer—strong, unyielding. It was that combination that forged a dual identity inside him, a war between the nurturing father he wanted to be and the stern figure he feared he might become.

"You're acting like I'm some sort of rogue parent. I just... I want to raise a well-rounded child!" he insisted, his voice rising defensively. The juxtaposition between their visions cut deep, and the roses of society's expectations felt like thorny reminders of the failings that lurked in every decision they made.

Sarah shook her head, frustration spilling over. "Raising a child isn't about molding him into something; it's about letting him grow! Can't you see that? Your own father was softer with you than you give him credit for, but you keep reverting to that strict model. It's like you don't even trust me to guide him!"

She stood abruptly, her chair scraping against the floor like nails on a chalkboard, and began pacing the kitchen. It was a physical reminder of the struggles they had faced as a couple: the way their own upbringings shaped their current realities.

The clashing philosophies felt particularly poignant this evening. Society had painted their canvas with narrow strokes, depicting what a "good parent" should look like, an unsaid list of criteria they both felt trapped by. The pressures of achievement, the incessant fear of failure—not just as parents but as individuals—loomed like a pernicious shadow.

"Of course I trust you! Just because I don't agree with you doesn't mean I don't value your opinion!" Alex shot back, a mixture of anger and desperation flooding his tone. His heart thudded against his ribcage, each pulse demanding he find a way to communicate without unwinding further.

“Then why do you always bring up what you think he should be doing, instead of listening to what he actually wants? It's like you're constantly waiting for him to fail before you can step in,” Sarah countered, halting in her tracks to face him.

Her hands were on her hips, the urge to flee the scene that seemed inevitable prickling at the edges of her consciousness. She, too, felt the urge to retreat, to find comfort in the solitude of her own thoughts—but she knew they had to battle through this, to excavate the truth beneath these swirling emotions.

Alex felt the heat rising within him, but underneath the anger was a wellspring of fear. He didn't want to repeat the same patterns that had shadowed his childhood.

“But what good is exploration if it leads to disaster? You know what your dad did to your brother in the name of ‘adventure’! Do you really want to take that risk?” As the words spilled from his lips, Alex immediately recognized them as a sincere attempt at calling out the past—a past he wasn't wholly sure he could escape from.

It was then that Sarah's expression softened, the sharp edges of her anger giving way to understanding. "And what if I want him to learn through his mistakes? What if that disaster is what helps him understand the world? The way your parents raised you—yes, it shaped you, but it also came with its pitfalls. We can't go back there, Alex! We can't let fear control our parenting!"

The roses in the room seemed to wilt in that moment, as if society's expectations wrapped around them like a noose, squeezing away the vibrancy of their love. It felt as though every societal pressure they encountered had been stamped into their relationship, creating a façade of what parenthood should be.

Silence filled the space between them, heavy and foreboding. It held the weight of their shared dreams, hopes, and the poignant realization that they were indeed struggling for control amongst the unyielding thorny expectations. Alex avoided eye contact, his gaze drifting to their son's crayon-enhanced drawings plastered on the refrigerator, a testament to innocence amidst the chaos.

“I just want him to have the best life—a life where he feels safe to be himself without the risk of rebuke,” Alex whispered, his voice now tinged with vulnerability rather than defiance. He could hear the echo of the love his father had enveloped him in as a child, the admiration far outweighing the strict lessons endured.

“But at what cost, Alex?” Sarah pressed, her voice hushed, seeking to soften the edges yet again. “Is it worth sacrificing his happiness while you mold him? Or do you want him to truly feel free to explore? Just think!”

In that moment, the wall dividing them began to break, each fragment peeling back to reveal fears lying beneath their passionate entrenchments. They were not opposing forces, but two individuals yearning for the same goal, tethered by the conflicting tapestries of their upbringing.

Alex took a deep breath, the warmth of the kitchen now feeling like it was enveloping him in a revelation. Perhaps this argument wasn't just a clash; it was a turning point.

"You know, it's hard for me to trust a world where I have to let him go. I don't know what that looks like when I watch him venture beyond our confines. The risks terrify me," he confessed, realization creeping in like dawn.

"I feel the same way sometimes, especially when I think of how the world can act; it's unpredictable, and it's terrifying," Sarah nodded, her eyes softening once again; the air between them felt charged with the electricity of newfound understanding. "But I believe in kindness and letting him decide how to navigate it—like your father taught you to nurture your concerns instead of stifling them."

The roses outside seemed to bloom again, their colors vibrant against the fading light; the harsh pressures attributed to society shifted into a backdrop instead of a glaring spotlight.

As the tension between them started to dissipate, the vision of their shared hopes began to re-emerge, gently wrapped in the threads of compassion and understanding.

Together, they confronted their fears, recognizing the need to integrate both their styles of parenting instead of declaring war on each other's philosophies.

"I don't want to diminish your approach. It matters to me. Can we try to integrate? Balance nurturing with what is necessary for his growth, rather than seeing it as a competition?" Alex suggested tentatively, pride swelling as he observed Sarah's posture begin to ease.

"Absolutely. I don't want to fight about this anymore. All I want is for him to thrive."

With those heartfelt words spoken, their shared laughter began to permeate the kitchen, echoing around the walls that had felt so constricting moments before.

Alex picked up a crayon-scrawled drawing from the table, depicting a massive sun shining down on stick figures—a cherished portrayal of innocence and unbridled joy. "Maybe we can let him help us decide which flowers to plant in this garden of ours, the roses and the wildflowers, nurturing them together in our unique ways. Yeah?" He was careful but hopeful, as though the world outside might reflect the new beginnings burgeoned from this very moment.

"I like that. Together, we can embrace both the roses and the wildflowers," Sarah smiled, warmth radiating through the kitchen once more. "We each have strengths to offer. It's time we recognize the beauty in our differences."

And so, the conversation shifted—a budding critique of not only their parenting styles but the realization of how intertwined their aspirations were. As they stepped away from the argument, they embraced the spectrum of love their family symbolized: a tapestry of nurturing ideals woven delicately alongside the need for guidelines.

As the light faded gently into twilight, Alex took Sarah's hand in his, feeling the warmth and support that promised to guide them through this journey together. No longer were they at odds; they'd emerged from the confrontation hand in hand, ready to navigate the unknown paths of fatherhood and motherhood—not separately, but as one.

And, slowly, perhaps even unexpectedly, the quarrel emerged as a crucial turning point, culminating around ideas of love, understanding, and unity amid the thorns of honest disagreement.

Behind the scenes of their lives—above the whispers of societal expectations—they were learning to create their garden where both roses and wildflowers might bloom alike.

Navigating Society's Expectations

Alex sat on the edge of their bed, hands clasped together as he stared at the wall across from him. The echoes of laughter filtered through the half-open window, his son playing outside with the neighborhood boys. It always amazed him how the simplest sounds—a child's giggle, the rustle of leaves—could stir a sense of unease in his chest. Yet, there it was, a constant reminder of the weight he bore as a father, an ever-looming question: Am I doing this right?

His wife, Jenna, walked into the room with a basket full of freshly laundered clothes. She looked up, her brow slightly furrowed. "You okay? You seem distant."

He sighed, running a hand through his hair. "Just thinking about our parenting style, I guess. Sometimes I feel like I'm caught between what I want to be and what I think society expects from me."

Jenna put the basket down and sat beside him. "You know, it's a conversation we've had before. It's not about fitting into society's box, Alex. It's about what feels right for us and for our son."

Her words were comforting, yet they felt insufficient to assuage the storm brewing inside him. "But isn't there some truth to what society expects? I mean, look at how it shaped our fathers. Your dad was always about toughness. Mine? He was nurturing, but sometimes I wonder if he was too soft. What if I end up repeating their mistakes?"

Jenna crossed her arms, her voice firm yet soft. "That's the thing, right? Our fathers were products of their time. We don't have to replicate their journeys. We can forge our own paths."

Alex turned to her, searching her face for understanding. "But what if that path leads us to failure? There's pressure out there, Jenna. That pressure to provide, to discipline, to be the 'perfect dad' who balances toughness with love. I feel like I'm failing before I even begin."

The sun had begun to dip lower in the sky, casting a warm glow that pulsed like the emotions churning within him. Jenna leaned closer, her hand resting gently on his knee. "The truth is, those societal expectations are often conflicting. Do we honor tradition, or do we break free for the sake of our child? It's a real struggle, but that struggle is part of what makes us good parents. We're actively choosing, you know?"

He pondered her words, aware they came from a place of deep reflection. They often discussed the norms that surrounded them, the unspoken rules of fatherhood that influenced their choices. He thought of how every male figure in his life, from his father to his friends' dads, had embodied extreme versions of masculinity. His father had been the epitome of caring yet stringent parenting. He recalled the countless times he had felt judged for his wishy-washy moments of vulnerability.

Conversely, Jenna's father had wielded iron-fisted discipline, her mother often drowned in the quiet turmoil of unmet expectations. This cocktail of experiences brewed a unique concoction of fear and aspiration within Alex.

"When I see all those fathers coaching Little League or taking control of their families, I can't help but feel like I should be more decisive, more directive. I want to shield our son from failure, protect him from becoming soft like I felt sometimes. But at what cost? Am I just throwing away the softness my father valued?" He furrowed his brow, the conflicting sentiments igniting a simmering frustration.

The tensions within him mirrored societal teachings that seemed paradoxical. To be a man was to be strong, but then strength also meant being open and nurturing. It left Alex in a state of flux, uneasy with the contradictions that forced him to reassess identity constantly.

Jenna responded gently. "Maybe the issue isn't about being or choosing one way or another. Maybe it's about embracing the fluidity of it all. Strength can manifest as vulnerability, and nurturing can be powerful in its own right."

He considered this, the notion of balance, of fluidity, resonating with him. Yet its practicality escaped him in stressful moments when he felt the rush of societal expectations rush upon him like a relentless tide. Was it instinct or pressure that led him to frame his parenting approach around rigid models?

"I've watched fathers navigate these waters effortlessly, and I can't help but feel envious," Alex admitted, a hint of bitterness in his voice.

Jenna shook her head, her expression a blend of understanding and frustration. "That's the thing, though. You only see snippets of their lives. You don't see their struggle, the doubts that plague them. All fathers have insecurities, Alex. It's human. The difference lies in how we channel them."

Her logic seemed clear, yet the cluttered thoughts vying for space in his mind stifled any coherent response. "But why is it that whenever I try to talk about emotions or vulnerability, people either look at me weird or roll their eyes?"

Jenna gave a small laugh, warm despite the gravity of the topic. "Because they've been conditioned to reduce masculinity to being tough and stoic. Society's view is as heavy as a ton of bricks. But the truth? Emotional intelligence isn't a weakness; it's a strength. Don't shy away from it just because others are stuck in tradition."

Easier said than done, he thought. The conversation they were having wasn't new. They had waxed poetic about the roles their fathers had played in shaping their identities countless times, but Alex still felt inadequate.

In the days that followed, Alex found himself replaying the conversations he and Jenna had shared. The duality of their upbringings gnawed at him. There were moments where Jenna's disposition reflected a side of him he craved to embody, and he admired her approach to discussions with their son. But still, a gnawing voice reminded him of the disparity between admiration and personal practice.

On a particularly sunny afternoon, Alex found himself at a family barbecue hosted by a friend, a successful entrepreneur and father of three. The atmosphere was lively, filled with the hum of laughter and the clinks of glasses. He noticed how his friend navigated the gathering, effortlessly commanding attention with anecdotes of family adventures and parenting wisdom.

Alex caught himself falling into comparisons as the evening wore on. Several fathers gathered around, boasting about their children's achievements, their parenting choices, and, most importantly, how they 'controlled' their households. The bravado made his stomach churn. Underneath their banter lay a tacit foundation of competition that left him unsettled. The pressure was palpable. He masked his discomfort with small talk, but as he laughed along, he felt like a marionette, strings tugged by societal norms he vowed to resist.

Suddenly, someone turned to Alex, asking about his own parenting style. Underneath the jovial atmosphere, a shiver of anxiety coursed through him. He felt the eyes of the father's circle scrutinizing him, probing him for validation. The question felt laced with expectation, and it was not lost on him that a wrong answer might lead them to judge him as nontraditional, or even worse—soft.

"Well, we..." he stammered, searching for words amidst panic. "We try to encourage creativity, you know? Not everything has to be about competition. I want my son to be... well-rounded."

He could see a palpable change in body language. A couple of fathers raised their eyebrows. Someone chuckled, almost derisively. The collective energy shifted, and suddenly, he felt small. This was the very essence of the societal expectations he grappled with daily: equating strength to control and competition.

A knot twisted in his stomach as small talk resumed, but his mind was still spinning in disbelief.

Later that evening, when he got home, he unloaded the weight of the day onto Jenna. She sat with him at the kitchen table, her earlier wisdom faintly echoing in the confines of his mind. His frustrations and feelings of incompetence poured out like a broken dam. "I hate the expectations. They're suffocating. It feels like I have to fit into this perfect mold of what a father should be—someone who's always tough, always winning, always in control. It makes me feel inadequate."

Jenna listened with patience, and when he paused, she took his hand in hers. "What do you want, Alex? What's your ideal for your son?"

He drew a deep breath, the moment for reflection swirling around him. "I want him to have a happy life, to know that he can be himself. But I also want him to know boundaries, that strength doesn't come easy. I'm just terrified of saying the wrong thing and having him falter because of it."

"Then embrace that fear as part of your journey, not as a failure. As fathers, we learn. Society doesn't define what's best for our family; we do. Talk to your dad. Remember the stories he shared about the obstacles he faced?"

Her words struck a chord, and Alex felt a flicker of hope igniting within him. He thought about the moments he shared with his father, how those conversations about life choices illuminated his upbringing despite imperfection.

In the days that followed, he made a promise to himself to reach out to his dad, to glean wisdom from a generation that bore different burdens and persevered through vast uncertainties. If he could confront his own insecurities and thread them into something beautiful, maybe he could begin to reshape his understanding of masculinity and fatherhood.

Days turned into a week, and finally, Alex found himself seated across from his father—a familiar diner in their hometown, two plates of pancakes laid out before them. The aroma of coffee filled the air, setting the stage for conversation.

“Dad,” Alex began, hesitating slightly as a cascade of memories washed over him. He could still recall how those warm, Sunday morning breakfasts sparked fresh conversations of vulnerability wrapped in love.

“Tell me about the pressures you felt as a father,” he finally asked. “How did you navigate it all?”

His father leaned back, a reflective smile spreading across his face. "Oh, you know how it was. I felt the weight of expectation every day. Everyone told me I had to be tough; that was the norm. But in my heart, I knew the values of kindness and love mattered more than the world realized. It wasn't always easy, but I chose to blend strength with vulnerability. I hoped to be strong enough to lift you up when needed but also gentle enough for you to feel safe."

Alex's heart swelled with the realization of how beautifully his father intertwined these ideals, crafting a legacy shaped not by societal expectations but by love. This was what he wanted to replicate.

The rest of the conversation unfolded like pages in a storybook, with Alex's fears and aspirations pouring forth, and his father's wisdom stitching them together into a narrative they could both cherish. He talked about vulnerability, about how it could coexist with strength, about how embracing emotions didn't equate to weakness, but rather, it paved a path for deeper relationships.

After sharing a heartfelt hug, Alex walked away with fresh insights shimmering in his mind. He might not have all the answers, but it was clear that societal expectations could no longer dictate the essence of his fatherhood. Instead, it was his duty to craft a new exposition—one founded on love, empathy, and a commitment to growth.

Inside, he felt a burgeoning desire to embrace newfound tenets, to redefine masculinity and fatherhood on his own terms. He wouldn't abandon the nurturing areas he valued; rather, he'd infuse them with strength shaped by experience.

Returning home, he found Jenna in the living room, flipping through a magazine. "How did it go with your dad?" she asked, looking up expectantly.

He beamed, an air of rejuvenation surrounding him. "We had a deep talk about it all—the pressures, expectations. I realized today that I can step outside that mold society's crafted. I don't have to bow to that rigidity. I can navigate my own path."

Jenna's smile lit up the room, and she reached out for his hand. "That's wonderful, Alex. You know, every step you take toward embracing your own definition of fatherhood is a step toward authenticity for both of us. Your path can be unique, and that's how we build something real for our son."

In that moment, the weight of societal expectations began to feel lighter, replaced by the comforting belief that perfection didn't exist, but love did. In his heart, Alex knew he would continue to face the complexities of fatherhood head-on, guided by the lessons learned from both his own upbringing and the moments woven within his ongoing journey. And as he settled into the quiet of their home, where their son's laughter echoed through the walls, Alex felt renewed promise—his own blend of masculinity, shaped by both tenderness and strength, was finally taking flight.

A Moment of Clarity

The evening sun cast a gentle hue across the living room, painting the walls in shades of amber and gold. Alex sat on the couch, fingers intertwined, the remnants of a long day weighing heavily on his brow. Across from him, his wife, Sarah, was organizing an assortment of crayons and papers strewn across the coffee table, remnants of their son's artistic endeavors. The air was heavy with unspoken words, the tension from their earlier argument lingering like a fog.

In that moment of quiet, Alex found himself reflectively staring at the ground, feeling the contours of the carpet beneath him as if it could ground him in the midst of his swirling thoughts. Their fight—the clash of ideals, the harshness of words thrown carelessly in the heat of the moment—had left him feeling unsettled. He knew they both wanted the best for their son, but why did it seem that they were so often at odds?

"Do you remember the first time we talked about our hopes for him?" Alex asked, breaking the stillness, his voice barely above a whisper.

Sarah looked up, her gaze softening as she considered the question. "Our little dreamer. We had all these visions, didn't we?" she replied, a hint of nostalgia lacing her words. "We thought we'd be this perfect blend of parent figures."

Alex nodded, recalling the excitement they had felt, the bright-eyed ambitions that had fueled their discussions during those late-night rendezvous in the dim light of their kitchen. The laughter, the planning—an envisioning of a path paved with love and nurturing. Yet here they were now, barely able to align their parenting philosophies, caught in a cycle of frustration.

"The nurturing I had growing up," Alex said quietly, "it's always pulling at me." The thought of his father's warm embrace wrapped around him like a comforting shawl, shielding him from the world back then. "And yet, I can't shake the feeling of failing to give him structure and boundaries. I see the way Caleb responds to authority, how he thrives when there are clear expectations."

"That rigidity has its merits," Sarah replied, her voice steady yet pointed. "But what I fear is the emotional distance it creates. I never want him to feel he can't open up to us. Like I sometimes felt with my own parents." She hesitated, her brows furrowing. "What if we end up just like them?"

The tension between them crackled like static, but it was starting to subside with every shared breath, every acknowledgment of their fears.

"I don't want that either," Alex admitted, his shoulders dropping slightly as the weight began to lift. "But I'm terrified of him not having the tools to face this world." A quiet acknowledgment hung in the air, one that resonated between them, bridging the pitfalls they had encountered.

Taking a deep breath, Sarah leaned in slightly, her eyes meeting his. "What if we create a nurturing environment that also has limitations? We can scaffold that affection with boundaries to help him grow."

"Blend our ideals," Alex echoed, the words tasting sweet on his lips. Hopeful visions fluttered within his mind. "We could have peaceful mornings, encouraging him to express himself, while ensuring he understands the importance of responsibility—like cleaning up after playtime."

"Exactly!" Sarah exclaimed, her face lighting up. "Like being strict with routines but encouraging those moments of vulnerability. We can teach him that he doesn't have to be perfect to be loved."

The dialogue began to flow between them like a stream finding its course, invigorating their spirits with each revelation. Alex remembered a scene from earlier that week; Caleb had drawn a picture of their family, a colorful array of stick figures adorned with exaggerated smiles, his vibrant interpretation of love.

"What if we encourage him to express his emotions through art?" Alex suggested, envisioning paint-stained fingers and joyful shouts echoing through their home.

"Art as a safe space!" Sarah chirped, her eyes sparkling with ideas. "We could have times set aside where he creates, talks, and shares his little wonders with us. That would allow him to reflect those emotions as they come, rather than burying them."

"That sounds beautiful," Alex mused, the faintest flush of confidence beginning to take root within him. "But we must also teach him that life comes with struggles and not everyone will treat him supportingly."

"True," Sarah agreed. "But instead of being punitive, we can guide him through those challenges—help him build resilience while feeling like he has us behind him."

"Deep down, it all comes back to love, doesn't it?" Alex's expression turned thoughtful as the realization washed over him like a warm tide. The heart of their discussions—their arguments—always pointed to that fundamental truth, almost as if it served as the north star guiding them through their parenting journey.

Sarah smiled gently, a genuine warmth radiating through her. "Yes. And love is not about being overly sweet or harsh; it's about balance. We're crafting a new narrative for ourselves."

As Alex pondered Sarah's words, he felt a sense of clarity rise within him; the discord stemming from their own childhoods had become less of a chasm and more like a bridge if they let it. They had both experienced the dualities of love and discipline, feeling the sting of disappointment as well as the warmth of encouragement. Now, as co-pilots of this parenting voyage, they had the chance to weave both experiences into their son's life.

"Perhaps we can even draft a parenting manifesto?" Alex suggested, playful energy threading through his voice. "A blend of our ideals—a guiding principle as we raise him."

"Ooh! I love that!" Sarah exclaimed, her enthusiasm infectious. "It can be the foundation we build upon. It will be a reminder of the paths we promise to take." Her hands moved animatedly as she spoke, almost picturing word strands made of gold weaving through the air, intertwining their thoughts into a radiant tapestry of parental identity.

Alex chuckled, the tension dispelled further. "It could be simple things: 'Emotional expression is encouraged,' 'Boundaries are essential for growth.' We can even write little affirmations, like 'Mistakes are part of learning,' or 'We always stand by each other.'"

"Exactly!" Sarah beamed, her eyes lighting up with each word, the exhilaration of shared dreams enveloping them both. "This way, we create dialogue around our parenting philosophies and keep the communication flowing. It breaks down those fears." It was as though their dreams began to take flight, the weight of responsibility transforming into a shared commitment they both desired.

As the cogs of discussion began to slow, an overwhelming sense of peace washed over Alex. This was not just a practical solution to their argument; it became a revelation—a moment of clarity that affirmed both of their ambitions as parents. They could learn from the shadows of their respective upbringings without succumbing to them. Together, they could foster a nurturing and resilient space for Caleb.

Later that evening, as the house settled into silence, Alex found himself in Caleb's room, watching him sleep. He wondered, for the first time in what felt like eons, if the parenting challenges they had faced thus far had brought them closer—not just to each other but to themselves as well. In the soft light filtering through the curtains, he saw not only a child nestled in the innocence of sleep but also the embodiment of hope: a child who would not carry the burdens of an outdated doctrine of parenthood.

The future felt like a blank canvas pressed against the palette of their beliefs, ready to be colored by their values and lessons, one stroke at a time. Alex's heart swelled as he leaned down to plant a gentle kiss on Caleb's forehead, joy mingling with gratitude as he whispered, "We'll find a way." As he turned to leave the room, he caught Sarah's reflection in the doorway; her smile mirrored his own, and suddenly it felt like they were both stepping into the same light.

They were both wondrously aware that challenges would still arise, that friction would continue to flare up amidst the beautiful chaos of parenthood, but they were committed to the journey. Together, they would navigate this evolution in their roles, embracing their differences as stepping stones rather than stumbling blocks.

As they settled into bed that night, a simple warmth lingered between them, a tangible promise sewn into the fabric of their hearts. They succumbed to the surrounding sense of peace. Alex entwined his fingers with Sarah's, squeezing her hand gently, a silent pledge that through every rising conflict and reconciling moment, understanding would be a guiding force in their parenting choices. They were no longer caught in the war of the roses; they were budding a garden of resilience, where love flourished in harmony with their ideals, nurtured by the shared commitment to rain down warmth amidst the chaos.

What My Son Taught Me

The Innocent Observer

Alex leaned back in his chair, inhaling the earthy scent of dried leaves wafting through the open window. It was a crisp autumn afternoon, and bright sunlight streamed into the living room, creating scattered patches of warmth on the wooden floor. Outside, he could see his son, Ethan, determinedly trying to ride his bike without training wheels for the first time. Despite the slight chill in the air, the enthusiasm radiating from the boy was enough to fill the entire house.

He watched as Ethan pedaled furiously, his little legs pumping the pedals trying to find their rhythm. The bike wobbled precariously beneath him, and a concentrated frown formed on the boy's face as he attempted to steady himself. Alex's heart raced with a mix of nostalgia and worry; the scenes unfolding in front of him ignited memories of his own childhood, echoing the support and encouragement from his own father and the uncertain moments of trial and error he had faced.

Just then, Ethan hit a bump on the path and lost his balance. With a small yelp, he tumbled to the ground, the bike clattering beside him. Alex's instinctive urge was to rush outside, to gather his son into his arms and shield him from the pain. But he hesitated, waiting to see what would happen next.

Ethan sat on the ground momentarily, his expression a mix of shock and disappointment. To Alex's surprise, he quickly brushed off the dirt from his jeans, stood up, and hopped back on the bike. A tiny, resilient smile grew on his face as he declared, "I can do this, Dad!" In that moment, Alex experienced a surge of pride swelling in his chest.

Witnessing the fearless determination of his son made him reflect on a pivotal lesson instilled in him by his father—a lesson about the importance of falling and getting back up. As a child, Alex had faced his fair share of tumbles. Whether it was learning to ride a bike or trying to speak up confidently in a classroom filled with older kids, the whispers of uncertainty would plague him. Yet, his father had always encouraged him to see these challenges as stepping stones. "If you never try, you'll never know. Embrace each fall, son; it's how you learn to rise," he had said.

As Ethan tried again, Alex caught sight of the powerful dynamics playing out. His son was surrounded by a safety net constructed of love and encouragement—an atmosphere where it was acceptable to fail, to stumble, and to learn through experience.

With every attempt and every miscalculated turn, Alex saw in Ethan a mirror image of his own youth, reminding him that mistakes were not the end, but rather a vital aspect of growth.

A few minutes later, Ethan found his balance and began moving faster. Alex's heart soared as he witnessed the sheer joy erupt on his son's face. With the wind in his hair and laughter cascading through the air, Ethan was wholly absorbed in a moment of triumph. The bike became an extension of his joy, a vehicle carrying him beyond the limitations he had previously imposed on himself.

This scene reminded Alex of countless childhood afternoons spent outdoors, falling and failing but ultimately learning to ride without hesitation. The tender reinforce of his father's embrace had made all the difference then, just as Alex's unwavering support was now creating a sense of security for Ethan. Watching him revel in success, even as shadows of past failures lurked in the recesses of his own mind, was a profound lesson in growth and acceptance.

As the days turned to weeks, Alex continued to see Ethan growing and evolving through various attempts at mastering new skills. From mastering his first soccer kick to navigating his way through difficult puzzles, each experience was a learning opportunity filled with missteps that flexed the muscles of resilience. Each moment exposed Alex to the delicate balance of nurturing confidence while allowing space for mistakes—a breath of fresh air in a modern parenting philosophy that emphasized achievement over effort.

One afternoon, they tackled a science project together for Ethan's homework involving a simple volcano model. With glue in hand, they set out to bring the eruption to life, envisioning vibrant colors and foamy, bubbling lava. However, the initial attempt proved to be an exquisite disaster. Instead of the expected explosion, a trickle of fizzled soda slowly dripped from the volcano's mouth, staining the tablecloth in a tangled web of color.

Frustration creased Ethan's brow, and for a moment, Alex saw the familiar flash of disappointment mirrored in his son's eyes. Memories of his own projects gone awry resurfaced, reminding him how critical those moments felt when aspirations collided with reality.

Instead of diminishing that hopeful spark within Ethan, Alex decided to harness it.

"You know, buddy, the best scientists in the world face failures every day. That doesn't mean they give up; they experiment and figure out what went wrong so they can try again. What do you think we should do differently?" he asked, his tone encouraging and light.

After a moment of reflection, Ethan's eyes brightened. "We should try adding more baking soda, Dad! And maybe less glue!"

Proud of his initiative, Alex nodded affirmatively, and together they modified their approach, engaging in a lively discussion about the properties of their ingredients. In that instant, Alex realized the magical transformation at play—that in nurturing his son's learning experience, he too was revisiting his own childhood lessons on adaptability and exploration. Each failed attempt became a stepping stone toward deeper understanding.

The volcano project evolved over several days, with laughter, experimentation, and reassurances guiding their efforts. The following week, when the beautifully crafted eruption finally took place with an impressive explosion of colors, Ethan's joy was electrifying. As the fizz and foam spilled forth, he jumped up, exclaiming, "Look, Dad, we did it!"

In that moment, Alex's heart swelled with a recognition of the deeper layers behind success. It wasn't merely about the ultimate explosion; it was about cultivating an inquisitive spirit, building resilience through engagement with failure, and embracing the adventure of exploration. Standing there together, father and son shared a profound bond, one which allowed each to grow and learn through the lens of love—reinforcing the nurturing behaviors Alex had admired in his own father.

Light began to fade, casting long shadows through their workspace. Gathering their materials to clean up, Alex couldn't help but reflect on how these small moments echoed lessons he had learned. The subtle grace of vulnerability, the willingness to adjust, and the unwavering support felt familiar, manifesting itself in the most unexpected yet beautiful ways. He understood that by allowing Ethan the freedom to make mistakes—just as his own father had allowed him—he was laying the groundwork for a resilient spirit.

As the seasons changed, Alex found yet another opportunity to witness Ethan's growth when they ventured to a nearby park for a family picnic. The sun was bright, and laughter filled the air as kids chased each other, their shouts stitched into a beautiful symphony of youth. While Alex laid out the picnic spread, he noticed Ethan wandering off a few feet, curious about a small group of children playing in the nearby sandbox.

At that moment, Alex felt a slight pang of anxiety—would Ethan find acceptance among kids he didn't know? Hesitation sparked within him, but he reminded himself of their earlier lessons on embracing failure.

“Let's see how he handles it,” he thought, an internal nod of encouragement.

Time seemed to slow as Ethan approached the group, introducing himself with his signature wide smile and innocent charm. To Alex's surprise, the other kids welcomed him, inviting him to build castles in the sand. Yet, amidst the excitement, Ethan faced a hiccup—one of the older children, eager to assert his dominance, scoffed at Ethan's castle design, causing his face to flush with a mix of embarrassment and misunderstanding.

Alex wanted to intervene, to rush to Ethan's defense. But again, he resisted, opting to watch from a distance as this moment unfolded. He had witnessed his father do the same when he faced challenges with his peers, and he understood that resilience often thrived in uncomfortable situations.

After a moment of pause, Ethan took a deep breath, his resolve shimmering through his initial disappointment. With an endearing spark, he replied to the older child, "It doesn't have to be perfect; it's our castle!" The determination along with the imaginative innocence behind his words seemed to diffuse the tension and redirect the playfulness among the kids. They enriched their experience and turned it into a collaborative effort, with Ethan as an active participant in the construction.

The moment encapsulated everything Alex had aspired to nurture in his son: the ability to stand firm in one's individuality, to embrace creativity, and to approach encounters with curiosity rather than fear. Witnessing Ethan navigate the complexities of social dynamics with the same spirit of resilience he learned as a child was awe-inspiring.

Later, as they devoured sandwiches coated with mustard and joy, Alex felt the profound lessons being layered through their experiences. Each moment of triumph and mishap fortified his understanding of what it meant to be a nurturing father. These shared occurrences, where Ethan was allowed the freedom to grapple with disappointment and practice assertion, were gradually weaving the fabric of a confident young boy, imbued with a sense of self-worth.

Days turned into months, and through various interactions, Alex embraced every chance to observe his son growing—daring to love and learn. Back at home, during everyday routines, he found himself reliving and reprocessing moments of self-discovery alongside Ethan. Simple tasks, whether it was making a new recipe together or doing chores, became fantastic learning experiences.

One evening, they attempted to bake cookies, the kitchen alive with laughter and flour. As they fumbled through the recipe, measuring out the ingredients, it was exhilarating to see Ethan fully immersed in the process of trial and error. After years of uncertainty, watching him navigate mistakes—a batch that rose too high, another too crumbly—Alex reveled in the beauty of each mishap, how they sparked joyful mindset shifts rather than frustrations.

"Maybe less baking powder next time, Dad?" Ethan suggested with an engaging seriousness that Alex found admirable. It was an instant where the father recognized the essence behind nurturing—trusting that he could guide without inhibiting, allowing a glimpse of independence to flourish.

Through humor-filled kitchen scenes and subsequent messes, Alex began to learn that parenting, much like baking, could often feel like a delicate balance of ingredients. While you needed a strong foundation of love and safety, what truly made the experience rewarding was the sprinkling of mistakes along the path. They were ingredients crucial to growth.

As the year came full circle, Alex and Ethan found themselves reflecting on the series of hands-on experiences—the bike rides, science projects, playful encounters with peers, and the shared kitchen adventures that compounded into a narrative of resilience and discovery that navigated deeper into the fabric of their identities.

Sometime in late spring, as flowers bloomed once again in the garden, Alex embraced a sense of pride in the young boy standing before him. Ethan's laughter was now more effortless; his confidence had grown, evident in the way he carried himself as he navigated challenges, turning every error into a stepping stone toward success. The lessons lived through their adventures were distilling into a well-rounded understanding of what it meant to be human.

One afternoon, they took a stroll through their neighborhood, the sun hanging low, bathing everything in a soft golden hue. Ethan, now brimming with self-assurance, pulled his dad into a local park filled with children flying kites. It seemed nothing defined childhood joy quite like the frenzy of colorful kites dancing against bright blue skies. With a look of determination, Ethan insisted that he'd fly the kite himself, sparking excitement and a gentle reminder of the thrill tied to an unpredictable outcome.

As they unfurled the mechanics behind the kite, moments gathered that echoed previous adventures: the delight woven in each tangible experience emerged as celebration, reminding Alex of those gentle nudges in his upbringing. Every moment created space for creativity, fearlessness, and the responsibility to venture into the unknown.

In the midst of the vibrant chaos, the transitions that had unfolded between father and son transcended the challenges of life. Alex's heart brimmed with profound gratitude for these melting moments where experiences coalesced into valuable lessons, embedding core tenets of resilience even within failures.

Finally, as the sun began to dip below the horizon, they revived the practice of savouring joy found in shared experiences—a renewed bond crafted in humility, reflection, and perspective.

Watching Ethan navigate through the vibrant energy of the park and revel in the success of flying the kite ignited the full circle of Alex's journey. Echoes of laughter intertwined with memories of past lessons were woven together seamlessly.

As the kite soared high above them, dancing and twirling in the late afternoon breeze, it symbolized not only his son's remarkable growth but also the brilliant nature of learning itself. Amidst all those moments of being the innocent observer, Alex discovered that nurturing a child was an art filled with nuances and layered insights, all rooted in allowing them to soar on their own.

Moments of Enlightenment

The sun hung low in the sky, casting a warm, golden glow over the backyard as Alex watched his son, Jamie, dart across the grass, laughing with abandon. The playful shrieks echoed against the fence, filling the air with a sound that was both joyful and liberating. Today was one of those rare days where the stress of adulthood faded into the background, allowing father and son to dive into the world of imagination together. As Jamie chased after a butterfly flitting from flower to flower, Alex found himself enveloped by a profound sense of awe.

Watching Jamie in his element, Alex couldn't help but reflect on the simplicity of childhood—the nearly effortless way in which a child finds joy in the world around him. It was a reminder of what had once been natural for Alex, but had now been obscured by the weight of responsibilities and expectations. For a moment, he closed his eyes, allowing himself to be transported back to his own childhood, where afternoons were spent in endless exploration, unburdened by the pressures of time.

"Dad, look!" Jamie called, excitement painting his voice in bright colors. Alex turned just in time to see Jamie's little hand reach toward the butterfly, his eyes wide with wonder. The innocence in his son's expression ignited something inside Alex—a flicker of hope mixed with nostalgia. In that moment, the weight of doubt and uncertainty that often clouded Alex's mind lifted, revealing an undeniable truth: children possess an innate ability to teach adults profound lessons through their simple acts of discovery.

As Jamie continued to weave through the flowers, Alex was suddenly reminded of a specific moment from last week during a playdate with Jamie and his friends. They had set up a makeshift obstacle course in the living room, a serendipitous creation born out of pillows, blankets, and their vividly imaginative minds. It was nothing less than a castle with a dragon to slay, a treasure to retrieve, and a grand adventure to conquer.

When Alex joined in as the 'brave knight,' he found himself embracing a role he hadn't filled in years, one that required engagement beyond mere participation. Jamie had handed him a cardboard sword, wielding his own with full conviction as he called out commands. "You have to jump over that pillow, dodge the dragon, and touch the magic wall before time runs out!"

Those words lingered in Alex's mind. Though he felt a flicker of skepticism about whether he would be able to keep up with Jamie's youthful enthusiasm, he surrendered to the moment.

As he launched into action, bounding from one pillow to the next, wild cheers erupted from Jamie and his friends, their delight contagious. Every little milestone of the imaginary quest was celebrated with joy, and Alex soon found himself caught up in the exhilaration of being a part of something bigger than himself.

One part of the course required crawling under a blanket fort—a seemingly trivial task, yet, in that moment, it felt monumental. The blanket hung overhead like the entrance to a hidden realm, shrouding him in a world where worries faded away. When Alex crouched down to emerge from the other side, he was greeted with the sight of Jamie's beaming face. "You did it!" Jamie exclaimed, his eyes twinkling with excitement.

In that innocent expression, Alex felt a surge of affirmation wash over him. This was what it all came down to—the acknowledgment of effort, the joy in shared experiences, and the beauty of a moment lived fully. His heart warmed at the realization that, while he generally took accuracy and competition into account in adulthood, Jamie's world celebrated the journey rather than a predefined finish line.

As the playdate continued, exhaustion began to creep into Alex's limbs, yet Jamie was far from finished.

"Let's do it again!" his son implored, clearly rejuvenated by the fun they'd shared. An internal battle raged in Alex. On one hand, he wanted nothing more than to accommodate Jamie's request, to shape the memory of today with a second layer of joy; on the other hand, fatigue urged him to call it quits.

In that brief moment of hesitation, Alex clung to the teachings of his own father. He recalled how his father would often bend his work schedule to accommodate his wants and needs—slowly yet unassumingly reinforcing the notion that love goes hand in hand with presence.

With newfound resolve, he crouched down, looked Jamie in the eyes, and said, "Okay, just one more time, my brave knight."

A grin broke wide across Jamie's face, igniting a renewed passion within Alex. They dashed back to the start line, the connection deepening with each repetition. Despite the weariness pooling in his muscles, the essence of being a father felt light and joyous with every candid laugh shared between them. It was not just a game; it was a bonding experience that filled both their hearts.

Later that evening, while tucking Jamie into bed, Alex felt particularly reflective. Jamie, nestled under his covers, looked up at him with those innocent eyes. "Dad, what's your favorite part about today?"

While Alex hadn't anticipated the question, the answer came readily to him as he considered the day's events. "My favorite part was being with you, seeing how happy you were, and sharing all those adventures," he replied, feeling the words resonate deeply within him.

"Mee too!" Jamie declared, his small voice a gentle sing-song against the quiet of the night. It made Alex ponder the inherent need for connection wrapped within those simple words. Reflecting, he suddenly recognized a powerful lesson: life's moments of enlightenment often emerge in the least expected interactions, wrapped in the joy and enthusiasm of a child.

This beautiful realization wouldn't only alter Alex's outlook on fatherhood but would serve as a poignant reminder to cherish the fleeting moments with Jamie. It was in these moments where patience blossomed into understanding and empathy—an understanding that each adventure, no matter how trivial, held the potential to teach invaluable truths.

Days rolled on, and Alex often found himself carrying this newfound perspective wherever he went. The vision of Jamie, with that bright smile, was a reminder that the true essence of happiness is often found in the connection shared between the two. Whether it was taking the time to read a story with Jamie at bedtime or patiently observing him learn a new skill, Alex committed to embracing each moment with gratitude.

One sunny afternoon, while on a trip to the local park, Alex witnessed a moment that made his heart swell with admiration. Jamie had spotted a group of children playing catch nearby. Without hesitation, he ran over, ball in hand, and joined the casual game.

Alex watched, their distance fading away as Jamie animatedly engaged with the other kids, a spark of confidence radiating from him. In that moment, he witnessed the innocent thrill of camaraderie—a world that thrived on shared experiences without judgment. Each catch and throw served as a new lesson about teamwork and the joy of discovery that naturally unfolds in a child. It removed the fear of imperfection, surrounding them with laughter instead.

The sun dipped lower in the sky, and soon the game broke, the children collapsing into heaps of giggles and exhaustion. As Jamie returned, his cheeks flushed with excitement, he opened up about what he'd learned while playing with his new friends.

"I didn't know how to catch the ball at first," he shared, "but they showed me, and then I caught it, Dad! It felt so cool!"

Here again, Alex found himself humbled by Jamie's perspective. Success for his son wasn't simply about making the perfect catch; it was about the journey of learning, the demonstration of support among peers, and the realization that mistakes were not failures but gateways to improvement.

"Do you think they'll play with me again?" Jamie asked, his little brow furrowing in thought.

"Absolutely, buddy. They saw how much fun you had. And you took the time to learn." Alex beamed at his son, pride swallowing his voice. "Just remember, every time you try, it makes you better."

Jamie nodded enthusiastically, a burst of determination sparking in his eyes. This commitment to learning reminded Alex of the joy inherent in realizing one's true potential through patience and perseverance—a lesson he had almost forgotten amidst the chaos of life.

As Jamie developed a newfound passion for meeting new friends, the innocence of childhood shone beautifully. Alex marveled at how simple moments brought profound growth—not just for Jamie, but for himself as well. Every experience became blended with laughter and the understanding that love was a journey forged in discovery.

Days turned into weeks, and the pillow fort obstacle courses evolved into imaginative games that traversed far beyond the confines of their home. Alex eagerly anticipated his time with Jamie, always looking forward to those opportunities when they fell into a rhythm of creativity and exploration together.

One memorable Saturday, they found themselves at an arts and crafts event organized by the local community center. Tables overflowed with messy splatters of paint, beads, and colorful materials.

Jamie's eyes widened as he raced toward the table, his face a canvas of excitement. A wealth of options lay before him, and within moments, he had concocted an elaborate idea for a project he wanted to create—a masterpiece that only a child could envision.

"Dad! Can you help me make a robot with these?" he exclaimed, holding up a roll of foil and a cardboard box. The urgency in his voice left no room for hesitation.

With hands immersed in craft supplies, they collaborated on building what Jamie named "Ro-Bob," a half-robot, half-vehicle creature that was part imagination and part reality. As they worked together, Alex often caught himself savoring the process even more than the end result.

"Look, Dad! Ro-Bob can fly!" Jamie shouted, holding the completed robot aloft, a proud smile dancing on his lips. The sheer joy radiating from him was infectious; it enveloped Alex with warmth, allowing him to reaffirm that moments like these were what mattered most.

"Of course, he can! He can fly anywhere with you, Jamie." With those words spilling out, Alex felt his heart swell with an even deeper understanding of connection and love—lessons that transcended beyond playful art.

Days passed, and the lessons Jamie unknowingly imparted began to seep deeply into Alex's soul. Moments of enlightenment turned into a tapestry woven with experiences that shaped their relationship. However, it wasn't until one rainy afternoon that Alex encountered a challenge that tested this growth in ways he never anticipated.

When Jamie returned home from school that day, he trudged in, droplets of rain streaking down his small face, mirroring the clouds that nascented overhead.

"Dad?" he asked quietly, his voice drenched in uncertainty.

"Yes, buddy?" Alex replied, sensing the shift in energy.

"I... I didn't get picked for the soccer team," Jamie muttered, his gaze fixated on the floor.

A wave of understanding washed over Alex. He could recognize that familiar knot within Jamie—a feeling he, too, had often felt in his own childhood. The sting of rejection loomed large in a child's world, evolving into a moment that could either create bonds or deepen them.

"Come here, Jamie," he said softly, pulling Jamie close into a warm embrace. Time seemed to stand still.

"It's okay to feel sad, you know. You tried your best, and that's what matters," he whispered, gently stroking Jamie's hair.

"I wanted to play! I wanted to be with my friends!" Jamie unhappily cried, tears spilling onto Alex's shirt.

"That's normal, buddy. But listen, sometimes, it's not about being chosen. It's about how we focus on our growth," Alex said gently. In that moment, he sensed clarity—a moment of enlightenment to pass onto Jamie.

"Can you tell me what you learned today at practice?" he inquired, seeking to draw Jamie back to the positives of effort.

Jamie sniffled and took a breath. "I learned how to kick the ball better and how to work as a team..." he trailed off, clearly focusing on the lessons rather than the disappointment.

"There you go, see?" Alex encouraged with fervor. "Those lessons will help you even if the outcome isn't what you wanted. Each time you practice, you build on what you know."

The corners of Jamie's mouth turned upward as he slowly started to understand what Alex was saying. "You think I can try again next time?"

"Of course! You'll keep getting better, and there's always next time." The glimmer of hope Alex saw in Jamie's eyes made his heart leap.

At that moment, the power of vulnerability enveloped their exchange and transcended the pain of disappointment. The warmth of their connection highlighted a necessary truth: life may not always offer victories, but the journey—the lessons we immerse ourselves in as we forge ahead—was where the true enlightenment lies.

As the weeks turned into months, moments like these continued to cultivate Alex's perspective. Through every teardrop, every laugh, and every shared adventure, he found himself not only discovering the intricacies of fatherhood but also rekindling the very essence of connection, love, and discovery.

Life would present countless opportunities to learn and grow, just like Jamie's ever-evolving presence in his life. And so, as days ebbed and flowed, Alex endeavored to cherish every fleeting lesson that unfurled before him. Each moment became a chance for enlightenment—a reminder that within the innocence of a child lies an inexhaustible reservoir of wisdom, waiting patiently for the world to share in its brilliance.

Embracing Vulnerability

Alex sat on the edge of the park bench, his gaze fixed on the playground just a few yards away. Sunlight filtered through the branches of the towering oak trees, casting dappled shadows on the ground, and the sound of laughter filled the air, a symphony of innocence and joy. He watched as his son, Jamie, stood at the base of the slide, a bit hesitant. The boys and girls around him climbed up the ladder with unbridled confidence, their faces lit up with glee as they plunged down the slide, their shrieks of delight echoing throughout the park.

Jamie, however, lingered for a moment, his little head shaking back and forth, hesitation written all over his face. Alex felt a tightness in his chest, an urge to leap off the bench and reassure him. But that instinct fought against another voice in his head: Let him find his way.

This was a moment of growth, he reminded himself. He could feel the tension between his instincts and his aspirations of letting Jamie navigate his own challenges. The paragon of nurturing his father embodied tugged at him; his mind conjured up memories of gentle back-rubs after falls, warm encouragement, and wise words of optimism that always seemed to be at the right place at the right time. In contrast, he could feel the shadow of his best friend's father—the disciplinarian who molded toughness through trials—looming in the background, urging him to push Jamie into the fray.

And so, Alex sat still on the bench, heart racing as he continued to watch. He settled for observing, waiting, and hoping. Eventually, the moment came when Jamie's resolve solidified. He took a deep breath, squared his tiny shoulders, and stepped forward, climbing the ladder to the slide. Each step was deliberate, his little fingers gripping the rungs tightly as he ascended, determination taking the place of doubt.

As Jamie reached the top, he looked down at the ground—an expanse that felt enormous from his height. Alex held his breath, waiting for the inevitable stumble or misstep. Instead, Jamie grinned, lifted his arms high, and swayed off the edge of the slide, squealing in delight as he sped down the slick surface. It wasn't a perfect slide; he spun a bit and landed unceremoniously on his side, laughter spilling from his mouth, bittersweet with surprise and delight.

Alex let out an involuntary laugh himself, quickening towards his son, who was already bouncing back to his feet. Jamie's eyes sparkled with excitement as he waved in triumph, brushing off the dirt from his shorts. He was undeniably cheerful, unfazed by the tumble. At that moment, Alex experienced the first prick of an emotion he hadn't expected: pride.

Pride blossomed from recognizing that Jamie didn't assess the situation through a lens of failure. His son viewed it as part of the adventure, an exploration and discovery that was simply a part of living.

In that fleeting moment, Alex decided to step back from imposing his own fears on Jamie. Watching his son embrace vulnerability illuminated a pathway in Alex's own heart. He chuckled softly and cheered, "That was incredible, buddy! You're a natural!" As Jamie beamed up at him, the world shifted; vulnerabilities weren't weaknesses—they were tapestries of experience that blended into life's narrative.

The rest of the afternoon became a blur of slides, swings, and laughter—a whirlwind of childhood exploration. But while Jamie reveled in his newfound bravery, Alex found himself spiraling inward. He was face-to-face with a profound realization spurred by each of his son's small victories. It was the journey of acceptance that Jamie embodied so beautifully. The courage to fail and adapt was a lesson not only in play but also a lesson that echoed in Alex's life as a father.

The memory of childhood struggles rushed through him—the moments when he, too, faced failure. He remembered stubbing his toe on the corner of the coffee table while racing around the house, a joyful chaos of boys during a summer afternoon. There were tears, certainly, but then there were also the hugs shared with his father—the warmth of understanding and acceptance. His father had a way of making every scraped knee feel like a rite of passage instead of a source of shame.

Birds chirped above, snapping Alex out of his reverie. He squinted at the sun setting in the west, casting gold and amber streaks against the sky. Something akin to enlightenment washed over him, and with it came a wave of self-awareness. In his own life, he had held onto the need for control, fearing that any stumble he took as a parent or in life would reflect poorly not only on him but on Jamie as well.

But perhaps, he mused, embracing vulnerability was less about exposing weaknesses and more about sharing moments of honesty. The thought resonated loud and clear. Accepting vulnerability opened avenues for growth—giving Jamie the opportunity to be brave also allowed Alex to process his own fears and uncertainties about parenting.

As the sun descended, Alex pulled Jamie close to him, feeling the weight of his small body nestled against his side. "You know," he said, "I watched you today, and I think you're very brave. Not everyone can just get up and try again after falling." Jamie's eyes lit with acknowledgment, and Alex continued, "I learned something from you. It's okay to stumble and fall sometimes."

Jamie's tiny hands clasped his father's arm. "Like when you lose your phone?" he asked with a giggle, dimples deepened as he teased.

"Exactly!" Alex laughed, imagining himself frantically searching through the house for his misplaced phone days before. "Sometimes we make mistakes, and sometimes we feel vulnerable. But we just have to get back up and keep going."

Their laughter harmonized, echoing in the fading daylight. In that shared moment, the vulnerability felt less daunting and became an integral part of their relationship. He squeezed Jamie close, a poignant reminder that their bond was ever-growing, anchored in understanding and acceptance.

Later that evening, as Jamie reluctantly knelt to brush his teeth, Alex sensed another wave of thoughtfulness. Each day they moved together as father and son was a new landscape to navigate—one filled with its own set of uncertainties. In the twilight of a perfect day, Alex realized he couldn't walk the path of fatherhood alone; he had to embrace moments of sharing, learning, and growing alongside Jamie.

They had both unfolded their stories against the backdrop of life's trials; failure and fear were bridges to be crossed together, inseparable from victory and courage. He wasn't merely a mentor or authority player; he was an integral role in this journey of discovery.

In the quiet of the night, after Jamie was tucked into bed, Alex sat beside him, watching as sleep washed over his son like a gentle tide. He marveled at Jamie's peaceful face, dreams flickering behind closed eyelids, reminding himself that parenting was a powerful cycle of vulnerability. Not just for Jamie but for him, too.

Over the next few weeks, Alex made a conscious effort to integrate what he had learned from Jamie into their day-to-day interactions. They baked cookies together; he let Jamie take the lead, opting to watch as flour filled the air, rather than taking over to ensure a perfect batch. When the cookies turned out lumpy and uneven, they both laughed heartily, another experience infused with the joyous energy that Alex had found in those twilight playground moments.

They painted together on rainy afternoons—canvases adorned with splatters of color that echoed the vibrancy of emotion rather than artistry. In those colorful afternoons, Alex shared with Jamie the vulnerability of creativity, the idea that not everything had to be perfect. "Even Van Gogh had his weird days," he chuckled. The laughter rang through the walls as soundtracks to their lessons learned.

Every parental misstep transformed into a lesson shared, and every moment of uncertainty opened a profound dialogue he had never imagined possible. With every stumble of his son, Alex learned to celebrate not the perfect outcome but the journey they took to get there—the messages of growth forged in shared reality.

Days turned into weeks, and the sunlight cast shadows across the living room floor, bringing with it a sense of warmth and hope. Vulnerability whispered from the corners—reminders that acceptance of their imperfections fostered a deeper bond.

One balmy evening, Alex stepped into the backyard, where Jamie was diligently attempting to fly a bright red kite. He watched as Jamie wrestled with the string, a picture of concentration and determination, shouting gleefully as the kite broke free from the ground, only to quickly plummet to the grass.

"You can do it!" Alex cheered, sensing the slight shift in his son's demeanor as he stood there, face grim with determination. Jamie squared his shoulders, resolute, and tried again—all the while, Alex's heart swelled.

What if he hadn't intervened with words of encouragement? What if he hadn't shared the lessons of resilience passed down through the warmth of vulnerability? Jamie's spirit shone bright against the backdrop of challenge; he didn't shy away from the act of trying again and again. Alex began to understand that this dance of light and shadow, of failure and resilience, parsed warmly through a shared vulnerability, was beautiful in both its chaos and its celebration.

Each moment stitched together a deeper understanding, and in recognizing Jamie's courage, Alex discovered a kindred spirit traversing through the ebbs and flows of fatherhood. He learned not just how to embrace his own vulnerabilities but to cultivate a safe space for Jamie to explore his own.

The days melded into a tapestry that reflected earnest simplicity—a raw beauty that emerged from the various threads of shared experience. Alex smiled at the thought: the process of exploration, mistakes made and triumphs celebrated, created a deeper connection than he had previously envisioned possible.

Conversations turned into moments of reflection. They would sit together at bedtime, where in half whispers, dreams unfurled before them. Vulnerability now felt like a shared thread woven tightly into their bond—one stitched with laughter and a vibrant understanding that their challenges wouldn't diminish them but enrich their lives.

One night, while reading a bedtime story about a curious little bear who hadn't quite figured out what to do when he got scared, Jamie looked up at Alex, his eyes wide and earnest. "Daddy, what do you do when you feel scared?"

Alex pondered for a moment. The question spiraled into the depths of his memory and whisperings in his heart. "Well, sometimes I feel scared too, buddy. Like when I started my new job, or when I thought I might mess up being a dad." He felt Jamie lean forward, innocent curiosity stark on his young face.

"And what do you do then?"

"I just try to be brave and remember it's okay to be scared. It's okay to stumble and fall—what's important is that we keep trying. It's how we learn." Gathering the courage, he leaned in closer, "Just like you did with the slide."

Jamie's smile illuminated the room as he replied, "So being scared is part of being brave?"

Alex beamed brightly, embracing this full circle of understanding. He nodded, pride swelling within him, enriched by vulnerability, acceptance, and joy—every emotion that came tangled together like the evening sky after a day well spent.

As the months passed, each day unveiled an opportunity for growth, and the bond Alex shared with Jamie flourished like budding flowers in spring. Amid the chaos of parenting life, they embraced awkward stumbles, shared laughter over kitchen mishaps, and navigated emotional uncertainties together. Alex reveled in lessons taught not only through words, but also through simple moments infused with authentic vulnerability.

This journey of acceptance was as much about Alex as it was about Jamie; it transformed both of them as they learned to honor the beauty of their imperfections. Walking this path of fatherhood became not just a title to carry, but a profound journey paved with love, understanding, and the sacred dance of life itself.

As he watched his son blossom into a young boy shaped by resilience, Alex realized that embracing vulnerability didn't make him weak—instead, it became liberating. It encouraged openness, communication, patience, and a rich landscape of lessons learned along this journey onward.

And so, with his heart filled with gratitude and understanding, Alex embraced each day as it came, and together they grew—an evolving tapestry woven together from love, laughter, and unabashed vulnerability.

Cracks in the Foundation

Reassessment of Success

Alex stood by the window of his modest living room, gazing out at the sun-drenched backyard where his son, Jamie, chased after butterflies. The laughter that echoed from his small frame stirred something deep within him, but it also kindled a question that had been nagging at the corners of his mind—what does it truly mean to be successful as a father?

As he sipped his lukewarm coffee, Alex glanced at the scribbled notes pinned to the corkboard above his desk. Each note represented a different goal or milestone laid out in the previous years. “Support Jamie in his studies,” “Expose him to new experiences,” “Teach him about responsibility”—all noble aspirations reflecting what he thought success should look like. Yet, with each day that passed, the abstractions of success blurred under the harsh light of reality, revealing cracks in the very foundation of those ideals.

The gaps in achievement that had colored his life stirred like shadows behind him. Memories played out like an old film—scenes of his own upbringing juxtaposed against the backdrop of this new parental role. His father, a soft-spoken man full of love, had always fostered a sense of worth within him, yet Alex's mind remained haunted by the unanswered questions of fulfillment. Had his father's gentleness defined success? Or did it create vulnerabilities that he was now tasked with shielding Jamie from?

He remembered the times when his father would catch him in an embrace during trying moments—a moment of failure spurred by a poor sports performance or an academic setback. Those hugs wrapped around him like a warm blanket, softening the sting of disappointment. Yet as he looked out at Jamie, swinging his little arms aimlessly in an innocent frolic, those moments felt increasingly distant, overshadowed by a more pressing emotion—anxiety.

Alex's thoughts shifted to his best friend's father, Mark, who ruled their household with stern discipline, demanding excellence without question. Mark's approach yielded clear achievements—his friend had been the star quarterback in high school, driven to succeed at every turn by the insistent hand of parental pressure. However, as the boys grew older, the emotional chasms widened. Alex watched in quiet dismay as his friend buckled under the weight of expectation, cracking and splintering in ways that seemed all too familiar. Although they had different styles of parenting, both men had left marks on Alex—one with softness and compassion, the other with rigid standards and boasts of success. Yet, as Alex breathed in the sweet smell of the lilacs blooming outside, he recognized that neither model was flawless.

In moments of quiet reflection, he felt trapped between the soft reassurance of his own father's nurturing approaches and the relentless drive for excellence embedded in the culture he had grown up in. Was success the accolades that came with academic or athletic prowess? A gleaming trophy? Or was it the depth of connection experienced in the shared laughter at a family dinner table? As these thoughts washed over him, Alex grappled with the need to define success on his own terms, forming a chaotic tapestry of reflections from fragments of his upbringing.

He recalled the exchanges with Mark—those late-night talks over pizza where his friend's father held court with established wisdom, all the while downplaying emotional articulation. “Suck it up,” Mark had said in times of struggle. “You need to learn to win in every aspect of life.” Words that had echoed in Alex's own mind as he now faced the challenges of his son learning to navigate failures at such a young age.

Those failures were becoming increasingly familiar: the crumpled homework assignments, missed social cues, and the occasional, yet inevitable, struggles with making friends. Inside, Alex felt a constraint tightening around his chest, a reflection of his quest for the unreachable standards of success. He worried about fostering a culture of resilience in Jamie while also providing encouragement and love. What if his approaches emulated Mark too closely? Would Jamie feel the distance that echoed through their experience?

At that moment, he heard Jamie's voice call out, laughter mingling with childish innocence—a sound so pure, yet it sent a shiver through his spine. Alex took the opportunity to walk outside and join his son amidst the wild grass brushing up against their bare legs. As he crouched beside Jamie, he marveled at the way every blade of grass was a new adventure, every splash of sunlight a reason for glee. It dawned on Alex that Jamie might not carry the same weight of expectations with him. What would success look like for a child untouched by such rigid ideals?

“Daddy, look!” Jamie exclaimed, pointing to a butterfly gliding effortlessly across the lawn. “I want to race it!” His little feet pounded across the yard, filled with joy and abandon, unshackled by the worries of the world—he had not yet learned the harsh lessons of performance nor had he felt the pressure of judgment that suffocated so many adults.

As they played, it became increasingly apparent to Alex that success in parenting was not a set of norms to follow but rather a living, breathing experience. Success was not how many trophies adorned the wall but was enshrined in the kindness exchanged between father and son. The realization hit him: this exploration of fatherhood required forging his own narrative free of the influence from those around him, especially Mark, whose version of success had begun to invade his thoughts.

The shadows of doubt continued to loom, however, and in moments of solitude, Alex couldn't help but wonder about the implications of his choices. He remembered the slightest tension in his father's fingers during moments of silence—the pressure of wanting to do well weighing upon both of them. He could see their shared confusion and uncertainty play out during many evenings spent in quiet denial, trying to connect through smiles that faltered when they thought success was measured in actions yet to be taken. Would he repeat that history? Would Jamie's laughter someday turn into silence beneath the heavy weight of unmet expectations?

"Success is doing your best," Alex whispered to himself as he helped Jamie collect wildflowers with trembling fingers. With each flower cradled in his palm, an ever-growing clarity broke through the fog of uncertainty. He thought about it more—he wanted to sculpt a framework infused with connection rather than pressure; to appreciate the small, fleeting moments as they came instead of focusing solely on the accolades at the finish line.

Yet a grappling conscious voice wondered whether this path could bear genuine fruit in society's eyes. "What will people think?" he pondered, thinking about Facebook feeds filled with inspiration from other fathers basking in the glory of their children's accomplishments. Would he fall into the hollow echo of what he believed to be success if he chose harmony over perfection?

That evening, after Jamie had been tucked into bed, Alex returned to the couch, draping a blanket over his shoulders like a shield emerging from the fray. He picked up a worn-out photo album from the coffee table—its spine cracking with age. As he flipped through pages of his childhood, Alex looked at the faces that illustrated a journey filled with love: camping trips with his dad beneath the twinkling night sky, fishing trips where laughter replaced the need for constant success, and wrestling matches that left them both breathless and light-hearted.

Each turn of the page rippled back through time; it was clear—those memories were embedded in genuine connections, not merely measures of accomplishments or accolades. As he shut the album, a realization dawned: he was in the midst of crafting his legacy, filled with all its imperfections and triumphs derived not from rigid templates but through shared experiences, dance parties in the kitchen, and gentle guidance on the swings at the park.

There was joy in watching Jamie giggle at the morning dew on blades of grass, and in sharing those simple yet profound moments of wonder. Just then, with a peculiar mix of clarity and warmth, Alex understood that success, in parenting, wasn't merely a checklist of achievements; it was the cultivation of relationships, the bridging of emotional divides, and an unrelenting commitment to be present in every moment. Every tear shed, every triumph relished wasn't merely a tick on the scoreboard but instead an essential thread that wove the tapestry of their lives together.

As the moon rose outside, showering the house in silvery light, Alex felt a profound shift within him. He wanted to be the father whose touch eased the burden of failure, who played hard but loved harder. He let his thoughts drift to the future, hopeful and eager to embrace uncertainty as a teacher rather than an obstacle. Jamie's life would not merely be a reflection of achievements; it would be an expression of love, vulnerability, and connection—an evolving journey sparked by the ties of their unique experience.

In the end, Alex knew that a reassessment of success stemmed from his willingness to unravel the pressures that sought to define him by society's standards. As the cascade of emotions subsided into a soothing calm, he realized that amidst the narratives of what success traditionally entailed, there was a hidden power in letting go, embracing vulnerability, and nourishing the bond that tethered him to Jamie. Here lay the essence of fatherhood—a journey yet to unfold, resting in the spaces between failures, gentle laughter, and the stunning beauty found within the cracks of imperfection.

Shapes of Conflict

As Alex sat in the quiet of his study, the familiar smell of old books and fresh coffee mingled in the air, prompting an avalanche of thoughts that had long been buried beneath the surface. It was during these moments of solitude that his mind would wander back through the corridors of his childhood, illuminating the shadows cast by conflicts that rarely saw the light of resolution. The echoes of strained voices and unspoken grievances played in his mind like a haunting melody, reminding him that the complexities of family were rarely straightforward. They were layered in meanings, filled with unacknowledged pain, missed opportunities, and the deep human desire for connection.

He let the steam from his mug curl around his fingers as he contemplated the patterns of conflict that had shaped his upbringing. His father, with his gentle demeanor, had always approached conflicts with a heavy heart and a measured voice. In stark contrast, the conflicts around his best friend's house were much more visceral, often flaring into storms that left emotional debris scattered in the aftermath. These experiences had left deep imprints in Alex's psyche, forming its own uneasy narrative about what conflict and resolution looked like within a family.

As a child, Alex had been a silent observer of the disagreements that brewed in the homes around him. He remembered many a summer evening spent at his best friend Jake's house, where the air would crackle with tension. Jake's father was a man of few words but assuredly charismatic in his authority, instilling a sense of fear with his silence that often gave way to explosive confrontations when expectational boiling points were reached. They would argue about grades, friendships, and aspirations with a ferocity that left Alex feeling like a voyeur to a volatile drama. The angry words seemed to hang in the air, pregnant with the weight of unfulfilled expectations. Jake would come out of those moments looking defeated, his bright spark dimmed, and Alex would feel a layered sense of helplessness, knowing the heart ache that lived just beneath his friend's hardened façade.

Yet, Alex realized that his own family was not free from its own set of conflicts, normally lurking quietly beneath the surface, only to emerge in small, damaging ways—such as terse dialogues over household responsibilities or subtle jabs about lost potential. These conflicts often lacked resolution; they flowed like a quiet river running just beneath the surface, creating cracks along the way but rarely bursting forth into the open air. They mirrored the dogged silence with which his father would approach disagreements. Alex's childhood memories were filled with moments when a disagreement over the smallest of issues—such as a misplaced remote or entertainment preferences—would slip into an uncomfortable silence rather than be addressed head-on.

As Alex reflected on these memories, he began to see them not as isolated events but as threads woven through the fabric of familial relationships. Each unresolved issue added complexity to the emotional landscape, cultivating an atmosphere where honesty became obfuscated by fear of confrontation. His father's gentle approach, while nurturing, often avoided stormy seas, encouraging an environment where feelings were not discussed. It was easier, he knew, to treat pain with kindness rather than face the conflict directly, but that choice left many truths unspoken.

In Alex's mind, the stories began to intertwine—his father's nurturing nature, which left conflict unresolved, and Jake's father's rigid authority, which transformed conflict into war. The layering of these contrasting styles of dealing with conflict became his underlying foundation, shaping his understanding of familial interactions. This cyclical nature of parenting drew stark lines of fracture in his own expectations of how to raise his son. Questions began to form, spiraling from within: Was embracing conflict part of a nurturing approach? Did calmness glorify avoidance? What was it that actually defined resolution?

To dive deeper into these reflections, Alex knew he had to confront the emotional distance built from these past experiences. There were moments he would revisit where the tension in his parents' home became palpable. Like the time his father had worked late, exhausted from long hours, only to come home and meet his wife's quiet exasperation—her disappointment in the unfulfilled promises of being present. A yelling match was avoided, yet the disappointment echoed in every shared meal, every whispered conversation in the kitchen. Instead of engaging in the conflict, his father chose to retreat—his retreat a double-edged sword, representing a kind and protective shield over his family but also a barrier that prevented deeper emotional connection.

Alex often pondered how many times his father's hesitance—itself a reflection of his own upbringing—had left unresolved tensions that gradually morphed into walls. What had his father learned as a child about conflict? Perhaps he, too, had been raised in a home where disagreements were deemed battles, to be lost or won rather than negotiated. Each generation carried its burdens, the baggage being passed down like an heirloom, unexamined yet easily recognizable. He could see the cyclical nature of this unexpressed emotional turmoil forming a loop, one that needed breaking. Each parent and child echoed back generations of rituals overwhelming intimate relationships like an unyielding tide: the need to be accepted and loved often clashed with human fallibility.

As these thoughts danced through Alex's mind, he found himself at the crossroads—the need to confront these layers of conflict and to break the cycle. The notion that unresolved conflicts could morph into dysfunction taking root over time filled him with determination. There was a world of difference between confronting conflicts and fighting over them; the former carried its weight within the realm of love and understanding, while the latter could fray relationships beyond repair. In attempting to define how to confront relationships with sincerity, Alex knew he had to draw from his own upbringing—cultivating the love and warmth of his father while dissecting the impracticality of avoiding conflict altogether.

Prompted by memories of moments spent in unresolved conflict, he allowed himself to dig deeper. He found himself reflecting on the tensions between his parents' differing perspectives. It was often his mother who steered the ship of emotion within their household, yet he saw, even at a young age, the struggle she encountered when faced with his father's reluctance to face discomfort. They were on the precipice of something richer, but moments where unity and understanding slipped away were much too common—heart-wrenching conversations often danced around the real issues rather than confronting them, anchored in avoidance and uncommunicated desire.

The dialogues inside his own home resembled cultural footnotes, echoing around tables laden with unspoken feelings and misunderstood intentions. The familiar refrain of, "It's nothing, I'm fine," became a rasping reminder that many conflicts rested unacknowledged, awaiting resolution ripe for the harvest of mutual understanding.

Alex knew self-reflection would be his weapon, fostering the potential for growth and deeper relationships. In examining familial dynamics deeply rooted in avoidance and conflict, he dared to imagine how much different life could be if vulnerability was embraced. He longed to give emotional language to the unsaid and champion a culture where all feelings—no matter how complicated—were welcome. Such realizations were a necessary precursor to the waves of healing that often rolled in the wake of difficult conversations.

He fostered an image of his relationship with his son—how he wanted to bridge these generations, crafting a legacy steeped in sincerity and honesty, opposing the inclination to sweep discomfort under the rug like hidden dirt. He knew that open dialogue would ground their interactions like roots sprawling through rich soil. To be present, willing, and honest would signal a shift in the pattern of his upbringing—creating an atmosphere of strength rooted in compassion rather than the rigidity born of expectation.

Instead of using the harsh edicts of authoritarian discipline that drove Jake's father's family dynamics, Alex envisioned a nurturing approach which honored those feelings, even the hurtful ones. He yearned to teach his son that mistakes were stepping stones to understanding—moments of learning cloaked in humility, where messy emotions could lead to clarity rather than conflict. This ideal presented an opportunity to recreate new experiences, transforming cycles of conflict into connections through empathy.

Through these reflections, Alex began to see the possibility for a familial renaissance, the chance to greet conflict with open arms rather than narrowed brows. Embracing genuine vulnerability could unleash a torrent of conversations that might resonate through generations. Each discussion could dismantle the barriers of the past, carving out paths toward healthy conflict where both sides were offered space to express their opinions. New rituals could emerge, rituals rooted in wisdom, patience, and a willingness to hear each other—that everyone could finally feel seen and valid.

In such moments of heart, sincerity would become the foundation upon which Alex could build, contrasting the experiences he had absorbed as a youth. His heart swelled with the promise that a healthier engagement with conflict could manifest not just for him and his son, but also for him and the patterns of life created, passed on through generations past. Breaking free from the suffocating hold of unspoken issues would lay groundwork for a dynamic familial tapestry rich with understanding, demonstrating that love bloomed best in the fertile soil of confrontation tempered with kindness.

As Alex settled deeper into those thoughts, he recognized that the bridge over the turbulent waters of conflict was layered with values—each layer signifying an experience or a lesson held dearly. It was an intricate road ahead, but it was one paved with hope; a road where familial love could walk hand-in-hand with the willingness to face discomfort.

He envisioned himself sitting side by side with his son, opening dialogues in moments of frustration or joy—expressing sentiments of hurt, disillusionment, or anger with the unwavering belief that it would lead to growth. In this infinite mentoring both father and son would grow, shaping a deeply rooted connection that would stretch beyond the bounds of mere existence.

Wrapped in the memories of the past, Alex understood that echoes of conflict would always be present, reverberating as reminders of humanity. However, he also learned that by addressing these patterns, he could not only rewrite his narrative, but also gift his son with a legacy of understanding—a legacy of parental love infused with the courage to transform conflict into a dance of compassion, rather than a war without an end.

Building Bridges

The sun hung low in the sky, casting a warm golden hue across the living room where Alex sat, his son's laughter peeling through the open window. Max was outside, engaged in a spirited game with the neighborhood kids, unrestrained joy spilling over in fits of giggles. Alex breathed deeply, attempting to find solace in a moment he thought would be carefree. Yet, an undercurrent of tension wove through his thoughts—a stark reminder of the conflicts that had recently emerged in his life.

Struggling to reconcile the contrasting approaches of fatherhood that he had inherited from his own father and his best friend's father, Alex knew he needed to forge a path of understanding. Throughout the past few months, he had faced challenges that made the fractures in his understanding of fatherhood painfully visible. The conflicts with his wife, Nora, sparked by differing parenting styles, rang loudly in his ears. It was time to confront those fractures openly, to seek a way to rebuild the bridges that had been weathered over the years.

Feeling the weight of the day settle around him, he reached for his notebook, the pages steeped in reflections, regrets, and dreams. He opened to a blank page: 'Building Bridges,' he wrote at the top. But in this moment of silence, he found himself at a loss for words.

Nora entered the room, her expression revealing a mix of worry and determination. "You look deep in thought," she said, leaning against the door frame, arms crossed. The sunlight caught the edges of her hair, casting a radiant glow as if illuminating the barriers that often clouded their discussions.

"Just trying to figure things out," Alex replied, scratching the back of his neck, a nervous habit he had developed when confronting difficult subjects. "I feel like I'm caught between two worlds, and I don't want our son to suffer because of it."

Nora walked over and sat beside him, her shoulders softening in response to his vulnerable tone. "You're not alone in this, Alex. We're a team—and sometimes, teams need strategies to work things out."

He nodded, appreciating her steady presence. “You know, I’ve been reflecting on how my dad interacted with me. He always made me feel valued, loved. But then I see the other side—the rigidity of Tom’s upbringing. It’s like I have two manuals on parenting, and I'm just not sure which one to follow.”

She reached out, placing a hand on his knee. “Maybe it’s not about choosing one over the other. Maybe it’s about blending what works for us, creating our own manual based on love and understanding. For Max.”

Her words resonated with him, almost echoing his own internal desires, yet there was a sting to the realization. “But what if I mess it up? What if I end up being just like my dad or worse… like Tom?”

“Then that’s where the conversations come in, Alex,” Nora urged gently. “If we open up to each other, share our fears, our dreams, we can outweigh the uncertainty. Let’s explore this together.”

He let her words settle like dust in the air, slowly drifting into focus—each thought crystallizing into clarity. He remembered a pivotal moment from his childhood, one that had formed the foundation of his emotional landscape. His father, with his unyielding warmth, had gently corrected him when he had strayed from kindness—a reminder that mistakes were merely stepping stones on the path to becoming a better person.

“Remember how my dad used to take time before reacting? It made me feel seen and heard. What if I try that with Max?” he suggested, visualizing the warmth of his father’s embrace and remembering the safety it brought.

"That's a great start," Nora encouraged, her tone brightening. "The ability to listen is incredibly powerful. You don't need to offer a solution every time; sometimes, just being present is enough."

The resonance of her words began to weave a tapestry of thought and insight, illuminating his path ahead. What were the words that defined Alex's fatherhood? What pillars could hold up the bridges he wished to build?

"Let's talk this out, like a strategy session," Alex suggested, a hint of excitement creeping into his voice. "What does each approach mean to us?" He grabbed a nearby notepad and began jotting down ideas.

"Okay, let's set the scene. I'll take nurturing values," Nora offered, rifling through her own memories. "For example, when I was younger, my mom listened more than she spoke. If I fell, she wasn't quick to offer a remedy; she let me express my feelings about it first. That made me feel valued."

"Exactly!" Alex said, scribbling faster. "And I'll take the tougher approach. I remember Tom's dad yelling about grades and sports. He thought pressure meant success. But I still recall the way I felt during those moments. It was confusing—and maybe even damaging."

Nora frowned briefly. "There seem to be two sides of the same coin, don't you think? Toughness brought structure for Tom, but at the price of connection. What if we flip that on its head?"

"By keeping boundaries within a framework of understanding?" he proposed, processing her idea into words, the jigsaw pieces suddenly aligning.

Nora smiled warmly. "Yes. There's no need for Max to feel threatened or controlled. Let him know he's loved—for who he is. Let that be our priority."

As they adjusted their sails, a new wind seemed to fill the room—a gust of realization, pushing them toward uncharted waters they would navigate together. The basement door creaked open, and Max ventured inside, his cherubic face flush from play.

"Dad, can we go to the park?" he asked, excitement bubbling over.

"Sure, buddy!" Alex replied, feeling the anticipation wash over him.

As they gathered their things, the air hummed not just with the vibrancy of father-son adventure, but with a renewed sense of commitment. Today, he could practice what he had learned: balance between nurturing and guiding.

At the park, surrounded by a microcosm of family dynamics, Alex smile as he observed fathers playing with their children, exchanging lighthearted banter and tender lessons. Each moment painted a clearer picture of what fatherhood could embody.

"Hey, can you push me higher?" Max shouted as he hopped onto the swing, laughter swirling in his voice as he swayed back and forth, his joy contagious.

Alex stepped closer, grabbing hold of the swing's chains, but he leaned down, lowering his voice. "How about you tell me how it feels to take off?"

Max paused mid-swing, pondering.

"I feel like I'm flying!" he declared, his eyes sparkling with delight.

"Flying, huh? That sounds amazing. And what does it feel like when you hit the ground?"

"Bouncy!" Max grinned, and laughter erupted. Alex pushed gently, feeling as if each swing mirrored his desire to push his son beyond fear while cradling his emotional safety.

"Bouncy sounds like fun! Remember, you can bounce higher, but you have to land safely!"

"I know, Dad!" Max squealed, his joy igniting deeper emotions within Alex—a gradual awakening of understanding from both the core lessons of his father and the grounding in mistakes that Tom's upbringing had highlighted.

As moments passed at the park, Max's laughter echoed alongside the laughter of other children. Alex allowed himself to relish in the happiness, sensing the threads of connection weaving between them. The fear that had haunted him, of not measuring up as a father, began to dissolve, evaporating into the warm air.

"You know what?" Alex said, reaching down to push Max lightly into another high arc. "Sometimes, I worry I'm not being a good dad. And I think I messed up a couple of times."

Max turned his head in surprise, the swing pausing momentarily. “What do you mean?”

“I mean, I sometimes feel like I’m stuck trying to be both things—nurturing and strict,” Alex confessed, meeting the earnest gaze of his son. The conversation, despite feeling weighty, was liberating.

Max pondered his father’s words, the expression on his young face oozing with wisdom. “Well, like if you let me try things on my own, I can learn!” his son proclaimed excitedly. “But if you never let me try, then I don’t learn, Dad!”

Alex’s heart swelled as the child’s insight washed over him. In his son’s innocent wisdom lay clarity—the bridge he wished to build was not only between himself and Max, but also inside him, helping merge the two styles of fatherhood into something uniquely their own.

“Yes! That’s it!” he exclaimed, feeling the last pieces shift into place. “It’s about balance. You don’t prefer cuddles over lessons, do you?”

Max swung happily, the rhythm of the conversation twinkling with joy. “I like both, duh!”

Nora approached, having been observing nearby, her heart warmed at the exchange. “Looks like you’ve just built a bridge right there,” she said with a knowing smile, pride lacing her tone.

“More like a skyway!” Max shouted, his enthusiasm steering their conversation away from heavy themes.

Alex laughed, sensing that hope and realization flowed freely in this simple exchange. “A skyway it is then. One that leads anywhere,” he mused, understanding the need for both love and guidance in the venture of fatherhood.

As the siblings wrapped together in a delighted dialogue, the sense of belonging grew—a thread binding them stronger even in uncertainty. It wasn’t just about avoiding mistakes or repeating history anew; it was about making choices together, forging a path forward that they could walk hand in hand.

As the day dwindled into sunset, Alex, feeling unabashedly grateful, mouthed a silent thank-you to the universe for the lessons learned amidst the rubble of self-doubt and fear. Though the road ahead would surely require work, he now felt steadied, a father willing to bridge the gaps with the love he had learned to give, enriched by the courage of self-discovery.

That night, as they tucked Max into bed, Alex reflected on how far they both had come. As Nora read a bedtime story, Alex sat at the edge of his son’s bed, enveloped by warmth radiating from both his family and the realization that building bridges didn’t mean erasing the past; it meant accepting it as part of their story.

Max drifted off with a smile, an image of soaring high in a world he would explore further, more boldly, wrapped in the assurance of his father’s love. Alex closed the door softly, his heart swelling with aspiration for a new beginning in fatherhood where every misstep could lead to new lessons of love and understanding, forming solid groundwork for restoring bonds.

In that moment, Alex understood that the work he needed to confront—repairing the fractures—was also the work of building deeper connections, perhaps forming even brighter paths ahead. Together, they would embrace the imperfections, hand in hand, ready to write the next chapter of their family's story.

Into the Unknown: The Father I Want to Be

Forging the Path Ahead

As the sun peeked through the curtains of Alex's modest living room, casting gilded patterns across the floor, he found himself ensnared in a moment of reflection. It was a Saturday, and the world outside was alive with sounds of laughter and the joyful shouts of children. His son, Mark, played in the backyard, darting around the swing set, a whirlwind of energy and delight. Watching him, Alex felt the familiar currents of nostalgia and hope intertwining, gently prodding at his heart and igniting the realization that fatherhood was not merely a role; it was an ever-evolving journey steeped in lessons, struggle, and love.

The cacophony from the backyard punctuated Alex's thoughts, each shout from Mark merging with echoes of his own childhood—the warm embraces from his father, the gentle encouragement that had always felt like a soft blanket wrapped around his shoulders. But as much as those memories were a source of comfort, they were also a catalyst for a nagging anxiety that crept into his thoughts. Would he be able to create that same nurturing environment? Could he bridge the gap between sensitivity and strength, finding harmony in the duality that defined his own upbringing?

With each passing day in this new chapter of his life, Alex was diligently carving out his identity as a father, seeking to synthesize the nurturing warmth he knew from his own dad with the resilience and discipline he had learned from his best friend's father. His experiences made him acutely aware of the delicate balancing act that lay before him—a navigation between harshness and gentleness, criticism and encouragement. He stood at the crossroad of his own past, determined to set a better course for his son—a quest for balance that shimmered like a beacon in the haze of his doubts.

Alex walked towards the window, watching Mark as he spun around in circles, arms outstretched, a tiny tornado of enthusiasm. This image ignited something within him, the ever-burning desire to raise a child who felt unconditionally loved yet equipped to face life's challenges. He longed to be the type of father who could adeptly wield a guiding hand, knowing when to offer encouragement and when to step back and allow Mark to stumble, learn, and grow. Embracing this vision, Alex began to solidify his aspirations into a tangible framework for fatherhood.

He envisioned a father who wielded encouragement like a sword, cutting through the blaring doubts that could suffocate a child's spirit. Mark would know that in his father's eyes, he would always see a spark of belief, an unwavering assurance that he could achieve whatever he set his heart upon. Yet, nestled within that love would also reside the necessity to impart lessons of resilience—teaching Mark that falling was okay, that setbacks were merely stepping stones leading to growth.

The notion of duality became a thread running through Alex's thoughts, weaving a rich tapestry of fatherhood where nurturing was not to be mistaken for weakness. Inspired by memories both tender and challenging, Alex accepted the need for discipline, not as a form of harshness but as a profound way of expressing love. Like a gardener tending to delicate flowers, he understood that boundaries were vital for flourishing, that they could help shape character and instill values that would last a lifetime.

He sighed deeply, envisioning moments yet to unfold—a time spent teaching Mark to ride a bicycle. The image came to life: he would start by running beside him, arms steady and firm, reminding him to keep pedaling, nudging him along with encouraging words. Then, as Mark began to gain confidence, there would be a moment of letting go, a conscious decision to allow his son to navigate the bumps of the road alone. It was within those moments, steeped in confidence and in the thrill of independence, that Mark would learn resilience; he would also understand that Alex's unwavering presence in the background was a lifeline whenever he needed it.

In the wake of these vivid scenes, Alex felt the rush of hope surging hotter through his veins. This experience of letting go would furnish Mark's memories with warmth, leaving an imprint that echoed both love and trust. But along with this intensity came the questions: How would he ensure that he maintained the correct balance? Could he cultivate an atmosphere where discipline married seamlessly with affection?

Those musings crystallized into vivid plans: balance would not only be a dictate of his actions but a conscious choice made daily. It was actually quite simple, thought Alex. Simple life lessons would be the core of this journey. Observing the people around him—other fathers at the park, listening to their stories and sharing a laugh over common struggles—he began to compile a mental toolkit. Each story was a lesson, a thread contributing to the fabric of fatherhood he envisioned.

During playdates at the park with Mark and his friends, Alex observed the tapestry of parenting styles unfold before his very eyes. The permissive father who allowed his children to explore, who seldom interfered when they tumbled and cried, created an atmosphere rich in creativity and exploration. Alex admired this dynamism, recognizing the value in the freedom given to children. However, he also knew it was vital to sprinkle in moments of guidance, the running alongside of children doesn't merely lead them, but ensures they learn to stand again, unafraid after a wobble.

Then there were the fathers who exuded authority, demanding respect through firm directives. During play bouts, they instilled competitive spirit in their children through rigorous encouragement, pushing them to always strive for more—a double-edged sword of motivation which made Alex recoil slightly, always wary of the fine line between constructive pressure and emotional oversight. He processed these contrasting styles, absorbing the lessons they imparted quietly as he envisioned the father he wanted to be.

Days turned to weeks and soon blossoms began to emerge from Alex's commitment to forging this path. Mornings shifted into fresh rhythms filled with laughter; he found new ways to harmonize nurturing with discipline. Every Sunday morning, he set aside time for "The Adventures of Alex and Mark," a series of imaginative and adventurous activities where they would explore the world around them—nature hikes turned into treasure hunts as they diligently cataloged interesting rocks or leaves impeding their path. In these moments, nurturing flourished in spontaneous bursts of joy and connection.

In the afternoons, he introduced a rule of 'five minutes of stillness.' During this time, Mark would be encouraged to sit quietly, providing him tools to regulate his emotions and channel his energy—developing an understanding of the relationship between action and calm. Alex would join him, closing his eyes and focusing on the sensations of the breeze, the warmth of the earth beneath his feet. Incorporating a balance of movement and stillness allowed the young boy to grow not just physically but emotionally, learning to appreciate quiet moments in a busy world.

And of course, instances of discipline arose, as they often do when children explore their boundaries. During one particularly sunny afternoon, after a long week of excitement, Mark began to ignore his father's requests to tidy up his toys. Frustration bubbled within Alex, memories of his own childhood experiences hinting at responses of rigidity creeping around the edges of his mind. But instead of succumbing to impatience, he took a step back, drawing upon the framework he envisioned.

"Mark," he knelt down, leveling his eyes with the boy's, "I know you want to keep playing, and that's important! But it's also important to help clean up. Together, let's make this a game." Instantaneously, their environment shifted; they turned cleaning into a race, with silly sound effects, laughter returning like a wave crashing on an open shore. His decision to balance firmness with playfulness left an imprint of mutual respect and camaraderie; a lesson learned not through fear, but through imaginative connection.

As those moments began to stack upon one another, Alex envisioned the future—a potential horizon shaped by experiences he dared to imagine. There would be the inevitable pitfalls of life, the arduous journey of growing up riddled with decisions that might sway Mark away from the principles Alex held dear. Yet, he nurtured an unwavering belief: the foundation he laid, built on love and understanding, would serve as an anchor during storms of uncertainty.

He began to draft visions of future milestones: the day Mark would score his first goal on the soccer field, elated and triumphant, knowing he had worked hard for it. But equally etched in Alex's heart was the idea that win or lose, he would be waiting in the shadows, poised with pride for the courage it took to step onto that field. He would be there, ready to celebrate victories or provide comfort amidst defeat—a constant reminder that the journey itself was far more crucial than the scoreboard's reflection.

Encouraged by the promise of what lay ahead, Alex initiated traditions designed to forge connections steeped in both joy and purpose. He set forth a monthly family day, where they would engage in collaborative projects, whether it was planting a small vegetable garden or creating arts and crafts at home. It soon became a ritual, blending the threads of labor with the joy of creating, sharing a sense of achievement together that fostered a lasting connection of love and teamwork.

As Mark dipped his tiny hands in soil, planting seeds and envisioning their growth, Alex sensed the power of these shared moments—they were the roots of the values he hoped to instill: patience, personal care, and the joy that blooms from nurturing both nature and kinship. Each time they dug in the earth, an unspoken bond grew stronger—a reminder that tending to relationships required effort, care, and consistent watering.

Through all these experiences, Alex began to understand that fatherhood was indeed a cyclical evolution of observation and learning. The amalgamation of ideals that once seemed disjointed began intertwining; his father's warmth danced alongside the discipline gleaned from those stern lessons witnessed in his friend's upbringing. Like notes in a symphony, the resonances of nurturing and structure were merging—setting the stage for an evolving melody that spoke to the heart of fatherhood.

Those quiet evenings spent recounting the day's adventures or sharing vulnerabilities now felt like threads binding together the fabric of their relationship—Alex's aspirations were becoming tangible realities. Today, watching the golden rays wrap around his little boy, who now wrapped tiny fingers around a delicate daisy, a sense of purpose settled into his bones. Fatherhood was about creating a safe haven for Mark to flourish, exploring without fear, fostering both his interests and his spirit.

Amid the chaos and unpredictability, Alex felt a ripple of assurance flow through him—a calm amidst the storm of challenges that parenting often presented. With each decision made in love, he knew they resonated deeply, shaping not just the son he was raising, but also himself. It became clear that forging this path ahead was not merely about aligning ideals; it was about crafting a living, breathing testament to the father he aspired to be—a embodiment of grace and strength, of laughter and lessons, of discipline wrapped in love.

As twilight sank into night, bathing their home in soft shadows, Alex turned to Mark, who was now nestled into his blanket ready to drift into dreams. He whispered a promise into the silence—a vow to nurture, challenge, and cherish, to embrace the chaos with open arms and a full heart. The path ahead was wide and looming, but armed with the lessons of his past and the dreams for their future, he would walk it boldly, step by step, as the father he was destined to be.

The Act of Choice

The sun had just begun its descent, casting a warm golden glow across the playroom. Toys were strewn across the floor, a chaotic illustration of a child's imagination wild and unbounded. Alex glanced around, the remnants of an afternoon filled with laughter and energy, but his heart was heavy with thought. Today had brought its own set of challenges, small moments that demanded more than casual responses. As he settled onto the floor, he reflected on the simplicity of being there for his son, while wrestling with the immense responsibility of shaping him into a good person.

His son, Ethan, was in the corner, building an elaborate tower of blocks. The young boy's brow was furrowed in concentration, his little tongue poking out in that adorable way that made Alex smile. But the moment was fleeting. There were other emotions swirling in him, the nagging worries that came from being a parent. How could he ensure Ethan would grow up confident, kind, and resilient in the face of the world's trials? Every day, Alex felt the weight of those choices pressing on him.

He closed his eyes for a moment, letting the din of Ethan's playful chatter wash over him. It was in these quiet moments of reflection that he found clarity. Alex remembered his father's gentle nudges when he'd been unsure—moments of help that felt monumental yet benign at the time. It was there he felt the roots of his own parenting philosophy forming. The love, the patience, the unwavering support that came from his father were guiding stars in the murky waters of parental decisions.

That evening, Lawrence, a fellow father from the neighborhood, had invited Alex for a casual barbecue. Alex looked forward to it, knowing that every conversation could unfold new perspectives. Sitting amongst other fathers, sharing a meal, trading stories—each moment was an opportunity, a thread in the rich tapestry of fatherhood that Alex was actively weaving. Conversations like these helped him confront his insecurities and revelations about his role as both a father and a man.

While at the barbecue, as they discussed the nature of discipline vs. nurture, Alex felt the internal shift begin.

Lawrence recounted a recent encounter with his teenage daughter, who had pushed back against a curfew. "I really had to lay down the law that night. It's important they understand boundaries. If we don't teach them discipline now, they'll struggle later on, right?"

There was an immediate tension in Alex's chest, a counter-narrative forming in his thoughts. While discipline was essential, he found himself reflecting on how it was delivered. Each choice in that moment reflected the kind of father he wanted to be. Would he be the man that encouraged harshness, or would he embody patience and understanding even when setting limits?

It struck him like a bolt of lightning—these discussions were not merely theoretical; they affected how he interacted with Ethan every single day. That night, as he recounted the events of the barbecue to his wife, Lucy, he realized this was ultimately about the kind of father he wanted to be. "I want to teach Ethan the necessity of boundaries, too, but I want him to feel safe enough to approach me when he crosses them," he shared.

In the days that followed, Alex faced many decisions, each small but weighty.

Ethan had begun testing limits in simple ways: refusing to pick up his toys, arguing about bedtime. Each instance ignited a fire in Alex's stomach. Should he enforce discipline like Lawrence? Or could there be a balance that honored being both a nurturing presence and an authoritative one?

One evening after dinner, Ethan refused to eat his vegetables, his frustration bubbling over into an argument that echoed throughout their small kitchen.

"You can't make me!" Ethan shouted, his defiance lighting up his eyes.

In that moment, Alex felt the pull of the disciplinarian voice whispering in his ear, threatening punishment or threats to take away privileges. But he took a breath, recalling the times he had seen his father navigate similar challenges—a soft hand on a small shoulder, a suggestion instead of a command. He knelt in front of Ethan, aiming to meet his eyes and to truly see him.

"I understand you don't want to eat your vegetables, buddy. But let's think about this together. They help you grow strong and play your best. Can we make a deal? If you eat them, I'll read you an extra story before bed."

Ethan paused, the fire in his eyes dimming as he considered the proposal. "Will you read the one about the space pirates?" he asked, intrigue overtaking defiance.

That simple exchange, that balance of love and expectation, made Alex feel alive. Choices mattered more than he realized; small decisions molded everything about being a father. They created pathways and laid foundations for Ethan's understanding of cooperation, and perhaps even compromise, as he learned about life.

Moments like these echoed back to his childhood.

Alex thought of how his father had sat him down once over dinner during a particularly trying time in school. The conversation moved fluidly from his struggles to his father's own experiences, smoothing the edges of disappointment with understanding. Alex tried to imitate that approach, and it became a successful tool in his toolkit of parenting. Each day brought fresh instances where empathy played a role in their relationship, teaching Ethan to approach celebration and conflict alike with open hearts and inquisitive minds.

As Alex continued to explore these small moments, milestones began to shift his perception of choice. One Saturday morning, a field trip to the zoo turned into a valuable lesson in compassion. Returning home, Ethan looked thoughtful as they chatted about the animals they saw. He recounted a conversation with a zookeeper about how keeping certain habitats clean was crucial for the animals' survival.

For them, it was simply one day at the zoo, but for Alex, it became a defining moment.

Ethan’s respect for the world around him was wrapped tightly in layers of love. "Dad, can we do something about the trash at the park next time?"

Those words sliced through Alex’s heart, illuminating the responsibility he bore as a father in shaping not only Ethan’s character but also his worldview. Such moments of clarity reminded him that each choice resonated far beyond the immediate situation; it echoed into the man his son would become.

Driven by new resolve, Alex began to weave more of these teachable moments into their daily lives.

He introduced community service into significant discussions, bearing the responsibility for conscious citizenship and ethical standing on societal issues. Alex felt empowered, confronted with his own act of choice in deciding what kind of father he wished to be as he guided Ethan through their shared experiences. They began participating in local clean-up days, much to Ethan’s excitement. Even routine chores transformed into collaborative adventures, bursting with opportunities for connection.

But it was not always easy; moments of frustration still surfaced, testing both of their patience. One such day, Alex returned home exhausted from work, eager to unwind. However, Ethan, brimming with energy, had other plans. He insisted on showing Alex the latest video game he had mastered.

As the evening passed, Alex grew preoccupied with his own need for idle time rather than engaging with Ethan’s excitement. The zest in his son’s voice became subdued as they ventured into the restrictive terrain of his fatigue. Soon, the vibrant joy that radiated from Ethan dimmed, replaced by confusion and disappointment. This situation forced Alex to confront himself—his need for rest should not come at the cost of their relationship.

Seeing the shadow on Ethan's face stung. **This was Alex's pivotal moment; the act of choice was laid stark before him.**

Would he create a perception of neglect or find energy within himself to pivot toward acknowledging his son to foster connection? In that instant, he reached for the controller, hearing his father's encouraging voice reinforcing the act of stepping away from his own desires for the sake of their bond. They played through the night, laughter filling the air as they conquered virtual worlds together.

Over the months, Alex began to compile a series of 'Milestones in Fatherhood,' small journal entries reflecting on moments of choice that mattered.

Each entry was a testament to navigating trials, learning from errors, and celebrating victories no matter how small, all shedding light on his journey towards becoming the father he aspired to be.

In one entry, he noted the depth he felt watching Ethan share his toys with a friend at a birthday party. It was a simple choice, perhaps forgotten by many, but the moment was overwhelming. A small act rooted in kindness could lead to enormous confidence in their relationship with peers, nurturing trust and fostering connections.

Another entry documented a conversation about fear. They sat together at bedtime, and Ethan voiced a worry about a new kid at school who seemed intimidating. Alex took a deep breath; here was another opportunity to choose to teach.

"You know, buddy, even scary people can be going through tough things. Sometimes, showing them kindness can change everything. What if you just said hi?"

Through every piece he wrote, Alex became acutely aware that **the father he wanted to be was no longer a distant concept, but a living, breathing aspiration.**

There it was in the labyrinth of each day, revealed in the layers of love, patience, humility, and compassion as choice played an intricate role. The subtleties of fatherhood had transformed into both a mirror, reflecting the kind of intimacy he learned from his own father, as well as a guiding light displaying the strength he gleaned from the wisdom of his friend's experiences.

As summer turned into fall, the natural rhythm of time allowed Alex to embrace both prepared and spontaneous moments. He found that while he had a vision for the father he wanted to be, forcing a rigid structure into that vision would stifle their growth. Instead, he began inviting unpredictability into their lives through spontaneous weekend adventures and unplanned trips to their local library.

One Saturday morning, pushing against the comfortable inclination to relax indoors, he suggested they hike to a local nature trail. "Let's see how many animal tracks we can find!" he had said, the beckoning prospect of an adventure casting aside his habitual need for control. In the midst of nature, amongst laughter and exploring, he felt alive; this balance of active engagement and pure delight truly encapsulated what he hoped for when he envisioned his role as a father.

As they trekked through the woods, Alex pointed out the distinct footprints in the soil. Their shared awe at the simple beauty sparked deeper discussions of the interconnections between all living things. He felt the values he yearned to impart strengthening through every conversation, solidified through their engagement with the environment around them.

In those moments, it became increasingly clear: it wasn't merely the choices Alex made; it was how each choice spoke to the kind of father he wanted to nurture within himself.

Every little action reflected an aspect of his emerging identity, and while he stumbled, he also learned to celebrate the practice of persistence. As winter approached, those small moments would echo in both their minds, establishing a foundation rich in lessons, love, and resolve.

By the time the holidays rolled around, Alex felt secure in the role he was cultivating. He spent evenings lost in reflection, considering each aspect of fatherhood. There was immense power in knowing that he was more than a passive observer; his choices defined him. Each decision added another layer to his fatherly identity, actions woven through time—a tapestry of love, resilience, and growth.

Ultimately, he understood the act of choice was one that would continue long past the challenges of these early years. His decisions today would reverberate in the man Ethan would become tomorrow, and as Alex danced with the complexity of that reality, he felt a newfound reverence for fatherhood.

Through practice and analysis, he smiled at the growing certainty inside him—he was becoming the father he wanted to be, one thoughtful choice at a time. In that journey, each step along the way, and every reflective moment only guided him deeper into the embrace of parenthood.

While the path ahead remained uncertain, each act of choice was now a beacon of hope, lighting the way towards love, growth, and the man he would continually strive to be.

Courage to Embrace Change

The clang of pots and pans echoed through the kitchen, harmonizing with the muted sounds of a cartoon flickering on the living room television. Alex stood at the counter, chopping vegetables with a skill born of necessity rather than culinary aspiration. His son, Noah, was engaged in a lively debate with the characters on screen, their animated antics offering a welcome distraction from Alex's racing thoughts. The rhythmic chop-chop of the knife became a backdrop to the swirling clouds of uncertainty that loomed over him.

This moment felt significant—not merely a routine task but a quiet turning point. Each vegetable that fell beneath the blade felt like a decision being made, a step taken into uncharted territory. The kitchen smelled of potential, but the weight of apprehension lingered in the air, heavy and palpable. Change was coming, and it felt both exhilarating and terrifying.

Alex paused, taking a deep breath and allowing the scent of garlic and onion to fill his lungs. The change he sought was not only in the food he prepared but in the man he wanted to be—a father who balanced nurturing with discipline, love with responsibility. The vision of the father he wanted to become had crystallized in his mind, but so too had the reality of what that meant.

Flashes of memories surged within him, like waves at the shoreline—moments from his own childhood and the conflicting lessons imparted by his father and his best friend's strict father. The warmth of his father's embrace often battled with the chilling echoes of his friend's father's barked orders and relentless pursuit of perfection.

What if he faltered? What if he replicated the mistakes of generations past? The worry settled in his chest like a stone, weighing down his resolve. What if, in his attempt to provide a balanced upbringing for Noah, he stumbled into the pitfalls he had always aimed to avoid?

As he continued chopping, Alex found himself wrestling with these fears. They circled his mind like vultures, seeking the vulnerabilities that lay in his heart. His father had been a staunch advocate for emotional intelligence, whereas his friend's father had emphasized results above all else. Both paths held truths, but navigating the middle ground was proving to be an intricate and daunting task.

Images of Noah's innocent laughter broke through the murk of Alex's thoughts. The way his son danced to the whimsical music on TV, the bright shine of joy illuminating his face—it reminded Alex why change was not merely necessary; it was vital. Noah deserved a father who could embrace complexity, one who could educate him in the lessons of both love and discipline without losing sight of connection.

The notion of embracing change flowed through Alex like a current—steady at times but tumultuous at others. Standing there, in the modest chaos of the kitchen, he was acutely aware of the delicate balance he needed to strike. With a renewed sense of determination, he set aside his fears momentarily. He could hear his father's voice echoing in his mind, whispering about the importance of progress through vulnerability.

Yet, the fear of inadequacy loomed large in his heart. What if he lost the grounding that had given him strength when he was a child? Would he be able to articulate love without crossing into the realm of leniency? Would the emotional connection he cherished with Noah become hazy, overshadowed by the necessity of rules and order? The discomfort gnawed at him, provoking the shade of doubt that had shadowed his own adolescence.

In his reflection, Alex noted something powerful: change hadn't just been about making bold choices; it was about observing and adjusting in real-time, responding to the ever-shifting landscape of parenting. Every misstep could guide him toward a deeper understanding instead of leading to despair. Embracing vulnerability was essential—it was through the acceptance of imperfections that he could discover genuine growth.

A smirk flashed across his face as he recalled the countless times he had tripped over his own feet in life, and how many of those moments had ended in laughter instead of shame. What if that same lightness of spirit became the foundation of his parenting journey? What if he could allow Noah the space to wobble and fall, knowing the best lessons often came from the exercise of trial and error?

The sound of his son shouting in delight—a triumphant declaration of victory over the animated villains on screen—brought him back to the present. Alex had a choice to make. And to transform his aspirations into reality, he needed to step into the unknown waters of fatherhood with courage and unwavering commitment.

He closed his eyes for a moment, visualizing the warmth of his father's embrace, the lit candle of advice flickering in the backdrop of his mind. "Change requires courage, son. Don't fear the fall; fear missing the lessons that come with it." The gentle wisdom enveloped him like a balm, dissipating the fog of uncertainty that clung to his spirit.

As he stirred the bubbling sauce, Alex felt his resolve solidifying. He was prepared to dive into the depths of parenting, aware that finding equilibrium would be a journey—one that would undoubtedly have its fair share of waves and ripples. Each choice to embrace change could define his path forward, shaping not only his own experience but also Noah's.

The back door creaked open, and Noah rushed in, his cheeks flushed with excitement. "Dad! Can we play superheroes after dinner?"

"What do you think?" Alex asked, a smile breaking through his contemplation.

Noah beamed, his small fists pumping in excitement. "Of course we can! I'm Captain Awesome!"

"And I'm your trusty sidekick, ready to defend the world with you!" Alex responded with a playful wink.

Laughter bubbled up, and in that moment, Alex realized that even amidst uncertainty, their bond was solid, rooted in the shared joy of imagination. Change didn't have to be fraught with fear. It could be an adventure waiting to unfold, painted with bright colors of laughter, exploration, and love.

Dinner passed in a flurry of food and laughter, a testament to the life Alex wanted to create. As they served themselves, conversations flowed freely, punctuated by bursts of laughter that echoed off the kitchen walls. Alex savored those moments, feeling the shimmer of hope mix with the apprehension that had originally enveloped him.

Cleaning up afterwards, he found himself reflecting on the journey ahead. The recognition that change would come with its own set of challenges was intertwined with a newfound appreciation for the adventure of being a father. Each decision, each lesson learned, each bump in the road promised growth, the magic of transformation at play—both for him and for Noah.

This undertaking required openness to the unknown, a willingness to not only adapt but also illuminate the path ahead with every step he took as a father. He had the strength of the tender lessons from his own upbringing combined with the fervent drive to ensure Noah would not feel shackled by expectations. Instead, he could become a template of possibility.

As the night wound down, Alex found himself standing outside on the porch, the cool evening breeze playing with his hair. The stars twinkled above, a cosmic reminder of the infinite possibilities that stretched out before him. Change, though daunting, also held incredible potential. He felt an electric thrill coursing through him, an anticipation for what lay ahead.

The notion of courage gradually shifted in him—it was not about the absence of fear, but the presence of determination to move forward despite it. He was aware that the waters ahead would be murky and uncertain, that there would be storms to navigate and waves to ride. Yet, the horizon shimmered with a promise of love, connection, and growth.

Embracing change would mean crafting a unique fatherhood molded by the philosophies he admired, and weaving them into the world Noah would inhabit. That nurturing foundation would ultimately empower his son, allowing him to flourish within a secure net of understanding, devoid of the harshness that Alex had so fiercely resisted.

Most importantly, Alex felt exposed, yet guided – grounded by the vibrancy of his aspirations. He was ready to create spaces where Noah could trip over himself yet rise stronger, where laughter outshone discipline, and values were not rigid rules, but fluid lessons learned through experience.

As he stepped back inside, he felt lighter. Change would always bring fear, but it wouldn't control him. It was there, lurking in the shadows, but Alex was no longer surrendering to it. Instead, he strutted on, embracing each unfamiliar step with an open heart and a vigilant spirit. He took a moment to breathe; he welcomed the unknown with a smile.

His son would learn resilience as much as he would learn comfort. Alex could shape his world anew, not by erasing the past but by integrating it into something unique, authentic, and joyful. It would be a journey from the shadows to the light, filled with bursts of inspiration, love, lessons, and the unwavering commitment to be the father Noah deserved.

And so, edge by edge, Alex began to embrace the change—a becoming, a transformation through courage—and he was ready to chart the path forward into the expanse of parenting that lay ahead.

Embracing Each Choice

The Symphony of Choices

As Alex stood in his living room, bathed in the soft light of the late afternoon sun, he could hear the faint laughter of children filtering in through the open window. It was a comforting sound, one that stirred memories of his own childhood—specifically, moments spent with his father. Those initial recollections were rich with warmth, love, and a sense of security.

In the chaos of the past years, Alex had often found himself caught in the cacophony of parental expectations, society's rigid molds, and the contrasting approaches of the father figures he had encountered. His father's nurturing touch and his best friend's father's stern guidance—two distinct approaches that had woven themselves into the intricate fabric of his existence. Now, as he stood facing the horizon of his own journey as a father, Alex recognized that every choice he had made so far had contributed to a symphony of parenting that was uniquely his.

Alex recalled the early days when he first cradled his newborn son in his arms, feeling both a rush of love and a tidal wave of fear. He remembered thinking about the kind of father he wanted to be and the ways he wanted to support and nurture his child. It was a terrifying thought, the weight of it settling heavily on his shoulders.

Would he embody the tenderness of his own father or gravitate towards the discipline that shaped his friend's upbringing? In that moment, standing at the intersection of these two legacies, Alex realized he had the power to compose his own melody.

With each sleepless night, diaper change, and midnight feed, Alex began to shape his parenting philosophy. He found himself reflecting, consciously and unconsciously, on the methods that resonated within him. He dedicated time to exploring tenderness, using warm words and gentle embraces to create a nurturing atmosphere for his child. The tender moments spent reading bedtime stories with his son—the sound of his little voice blending with the rhythm of the story—became the heartbeat of their nightly ritual. Quite often, he would recall the gentle embrace of his father, understanding that those hallowed moments were not merely memories; they were the notes playing in his mind, each one harmonizing to create a refuge of comfort.

Yet, amid those soft notes resided the contrasting rhythm of strict discipline. There were moments when Alex felt the pull of that tough-love mantra, especially when his son began testing boundaries. It was during one of these discipline practices that Alex's internal struggle arose, where he instinctively echoed the lessons learned from his friend's father. He remembered an incident in the playground when his son misbehaved—running away from him when called, laughing at the rules that tethered him. The impulse to react with strictness surged within him, fueled by the hope of raising a 'well-behaved' child. However, as he crouched down to his son's level, the compassionate words of his father echoed in his mind: "Embrace understanding, Alex. Love is the bridge to guidance."

In that moment, he made a choice. Instead of reprimanding his child with a stern voice, he knelt beside him, took a deep breath, and calmly asked why he had chosen to run. The response was an innocent laugh, a pure expression of childhood freedom. And it struck Alex like a chord resonating through a grand symphony—a moment of clarity that underscored the importance of connection in establishing boundaries. This exchange became part of the evolving composition of their relationship, blending love and discipline into the harmonious tune of acceptance.

Amid his trials, Alex also sought out the wisdom of other fathers in his community. Each conversation added depth to the symphonic arrangement he was creating. There was the father who proudly embraced a free-range philosophy, advocating for more independence and exploration. Alex observed how such an approach allowed his children to cultivate valuable lessons, discovering their limits and capacities through the freedom granted to them. Conversely, the stringent father reflecting traditional values provided contrasting insights. Alex took note of the sacrifices inherent in such rigidity, recognizing that even success could have a cost—an emotional distance that reverberated throughout familial bonds.

As Alex navigated the myriad of perspectives, he began to appreciate the nuances of each parenting style. He chose to create room for both the nurturing love instilled in him by his father and the necessary discipline shaped by his friend's upbringing. This realization led him to an epiphany—each choice incrementally contributed to a dynamic yet cohesive journey.

The juxtaposition of nurturing and discipline reminded him of the duality of music: the soft melodies woven with stronger, rhythmic beats. Alex embraced this duality, understanding that patience, kindness, support, and directives formed an orchestrated rhythm within his parenting journey.

It wasn't a matter of right or wrong; it was a matter of balance. As he reflected on his past, he considered the moments where unconditional love broke the mold—moments when he learned that the beauty of growth lay in vulnerability. The vulnerability of a father embracing his child's imperfections and frailties while fostering an environment filled with love.

Through countless sleepless nights and moments of self-doubt, Alex consistently sought to intertwine the lessons imparted by both father figures. It was not merely a matter of adopting rules or traditions but a crafting of an entire symphony—of values, ideas, and emotions—that resonated authentically with who he was.

He smiled as he observed his son playing outside, fully engaged in the joys of childhood, echoing laughter that danced in tandem with the warm breeze. With each interaction they shared, from silly tickle fights to heart-to-heart talks about fear and dreams, Alex recognized that his son learned from him just as much as he desired to impart wisdom. In those fleeting moments, Alex saw the ineffable blend of choices that scaffolding his relationship—each one forming a note, a phrase, or a movement in a grand orchestration of family life.

Life, he realized, was not a well-defined stage with distinct melodies and rhythms but rather a rich tapestry, weaving together the strands of love, uncertainty, laughter, mistakes, and joy into an unpredictable yet beautiful composition. It represented the endless possibilities of every choice made, deliberately or instinctively, within the journey of fatherhood.

Reflecting on his upbringing, Alex came to see that his father had not merely been a caretaker but a significant composer of life's events—a guiding artist whose nurturing spirit shaped his foundation. Alex understood now that it was those very values woven into his father's nurturing embrace that inspired his own commitment to fostering a space where love and understanding thrived.

Of course, struggles remained. Each day presented its own set of challenges, moments filled with frustration, the ebb and flow of navigating childhood's unpredictability. Yet, Alex felt less like a conductor wrestling with a cacophony of sounds and more like a composer embracing the complexity of an evolving score. On the firm realization that perfection in parenting was unattainable, he found solace in appreciating the journey's beauty.

As his son continued to play, Alex captured a glimpse of the future—the child he hoped his son would grow to be. He envisioned his son standing at his own crossroads one day, wrestling with choices that would color his pathway, needing the wisdom learned from his own father. The tapestry threaded through every lesson—each laugh, hug, tear, and conflict—would, in turn, echo through future generations.

It became clear to Alex that love wasn't just an emotion or a gesture. It was an intricate composition weaving together everything that had been taught, learned, and shared. The tapestry that sat at the core of family life was crafted not just from light but also from shadows—the moments of doubt and uncertainty that shaped their course. Each hue played a critical role, creating layers of meaning that elevated their experiences. The conflicts between nurturing and strictness, love and discipline, dissatisfaction and pride—these layers created depth in the melody of fatherhood, offering Alex resilience and insight into the multifaceted nature of human emotion.

As bedtime approached, Alex settled beside his son, the sounds of play giving way to the gentleness of transition into rest. They shared a familiar routine—storytime. He opened the book, the pages worn and familiar, and started to read aloud, his son snuggling closer. In that serene moment, Alex recognized the music within those pages—the lessons of adventure, empathy, and growth pouring into their shared space. This simple act embodied all that mattered in fatherhood—imparted wisdom layered softly upon choices made.

Through shared stories and vivid tales, Alex could weave together what he hoped would become the soundtrack of his son's life—a melody that harmonized laughter, growth, love, and connection.

In the embrace of stillness, surrounded by the soft whisper of dreams and hopes, Alex realized that each choice made, each moment cherished, formed a new layer in the symphony of fatherhood. As he tucked his son in, kissed his forehead, and extinguished the light, Alex understood that it was not solely about the symphony but the dance between voices filling their lives—that ever-changing, fluid nature of parenting. This dance would forever be in motion, evolving as they both grew, molded by the choices they made together.

With a renewed sense of purpose, he walked away from the room carrying a melody of love within—a song crafted through moments shared, choices embraced, and the realization that fatherhood was not a static performance but a beautiful symphony in perpetual creation.

Lessons for Future Generations

As the sun settled beneath the horizon, casting long shadows across the living room, Alex sank into the well-worn armchair that had been his father's favorite spot. Its fabric had softened over the years, much like the lessons imbued within its seams. He glanced at the photographs adorning the walls, each one a snapshot of life, love, and laughter, but tonight, his gaze settled on a single image—a candid laugh shared between himself and his son, Ethan, during a rare moment of unbridled joy at the park. This particular photograph encapsulated more than just a fleeting memory; it captured Alex's dreams for his son's future and the aspirations he dared to nurture amidst the lessons of fatherhood learned along his own journey.

Just as his father had done, Alex hoped to build a foundation for Ethan—one built on love, understanding, and resilience. He envisioned a future where his son felt secure enough to embrace his vulnerabilities, explore his passions, and navigate the complexities of life. The thought rippled through Alex's heart, bringing forth a rush of emotion. What did he want for Ethan? What lessons carried with them the weight to shape a future rich with promise?

Alex closed his eyes, the soft flicker of nostalgia washing over him as he recalled his own upbringing—those moments filled with laughter, sage advice, and, yes, even the occasional sting of disappointment. His father had been there with warm embraces and heartfelt conversations that transcended generations, encouraging him to dream, to question, to grow. Those lessons were the tender threads woven into the fabric of his childhood, a fabric he now sought to replicate for his son, but with his unique touch—a balance of guidance and freedom.

He opened his eyes, taking a deep breath, and began to ponder the values he wished to impart. The first came to him in a vibrant flash: empathy. In a world rife with division and misunderstanding, he wanted Ethan to understand the power of compassion—the ability to stand in someone else's shoes, to feel their joy, their pain, and to respond with kindness. Alex could envision his son as a young boy, perched atop a swing, comforting a friend who had fallen down. He could see Ethan leaning in, whispering words of comfort as he helped them back to their feet. That simple act would set the tone for how he connected with others, how he built bridges instead of walls, fostering relationships grounded in genuine understanding.

Following closely behind empathy was the lesson of resilience. Life would undoubtedly present its share of challenges, of setbacks that could threaten to knock Ethan off his feet. Alex envisioned a future where he could turn to his son, meeting him at eye level after a disappointing experience—a failed test, a lost game—and tell him stories of strength and perseverance. Alex would share his own failures, the times he fell short of expectations but chose to learn and grow. He imagined saying, "It's not about how hard you fall, but how gracefully you rise again. It's how you respond to the storms that define you, son. Choose to embrace them, learn from them, and you will emerge stronger."

With each lesson Alex nurtured in his heart, new images danced before his mind's eye. He envisioned days in the backyard filled with laughter, teaching Ethan to ride a bike, celebrating with him as he wobbled, but encouraging him to get back on the seat after a fall, to trust in his ability to master this new skill. Every push, every word of encouragement would serve as an affirmation teaching Ethan that every stumble was merely a stepping stone along the way.

He longed for his son to embrace curiosity, to seek out knowledge and new experiences fearlessly. "Adventure does not always come without risks, but it is in taking those risks that you find the most rewarding experiences. You must learn to explore the corners of your mind and the world around you. Be bold, ask questions, and never shy away from opportunities to expand your horizons," Alex mused silently to himself. In his mind, he could see Ethan diving into new projects, exploring from art to science, learning to appreciate the beauty of creation while recognizing his own unique gifts.

Amidst these visions, there was a clear thread connecting each lesson—vulnerability. Alex reflected on moments when he had allowed himself to be vulnerable in front of his father, how that openness had fostered a deeper connection between them. He yearned for Ethan to understand that strength lay not only in stoicism but in being brave enough to show his true self, to express his feelings without fear of judgment.

From these thoughts, an image of a memory emerged: a father and son, sitting side by side under the dim glow of a shared lamp, Ethan opening up about the day's struggles, a frown etched across his face. Alex envisioned himself responding softly, reminding Ethan that it was okay to have a bad day, that expressing emotions required strength, and that in his vulnerability, he would find a deeper level of connection with the world around him.

Yet with all these lessons to shape his dreams, there loomed an underlying lesson that brought an added layer of depth to his aspirations—self-acceptance. Alex had grappled with self-doubt throughout his own life, battling internal critics that too often threatened to overshadow his successes. He imagined encouraging Ethan to embrace his individuality and to love himself, flaws and all.

The picture solidified in his mind: Ethan standing proudly in front of a mirror—a patchwork of mismatched clothing, hair still a tousled mess, but a radiant smile lighting up his face. "You are perfect just the way you are, son. Always remember that your uniqueness is your greatest asset. Embrace your quirks and let them shine. Don't let others define who you should be."

Guided by this hope, Alex found clarity in what he wanted each lesson to root within Ethan: a strength that would ripple through generations, shaping the kind of man he would ultimately grow into. He envisioned a time when Ethan would share these same lessons with his own children, perhaps sitting beneath a similar lamp, sharing laughter, and guiding them through life's unpredictability.

In this living room, still resonating with his father's love, Alex felt a sense of calm wash over him. Every lesson shared, every hope nurtured, would draft a roadmap for potential future generations—each choice steeped in love, and supportive of strength.

Alex leaned back in his chair, a warm blend of excitement and determination rushing through him. He began to brainstorm ways to instill these values in Ethan's daily routine. He envisioned creating rituals that would anchor them in laughter and reflection. Weekly family nights filled with storytelling and games could become the backbone of a shared experience, reinforcing their bond, and providing ample opportunities for open discussions.

He painted a picture of outings spent volunteering at local charities where they could learn the importance of empathy through action. Their weekends might be filled with nature hikes and museum visits, fostering curiosity and a love for discovery.

In between the laughter, mishaps, and shared experiences, there would be moments for reflection, enabling Ethan to articulate his feelings and thoughts, nurturing both vulnerability and emotional intelligence. Alex imagined gathering in the living room again, perhaps years later, as he listened intently to Ethan recount challenges faced and lessons learned, each moment a precious thread in the beautiful tapestry of their shared journey.

As he lingered in the warmth of these aspirations, it dawned on him that this cycle—the cycle of love, learning, and reflecting—extended far beyond himself. With every lesson he offered Ethan, he was contributing to a legacy, a tradition of fatherhood that challenged the norms of what it meant to be a parent, nurturing growth instead of striving for perfection. This very notion brought about a sense of peace.

In this understanding was a profound realization—each choice made today would steer not only Ethan's life but the lives of those who would come after him. Success wouldn't be defined by accolades or achievements but by the emotional foundation anchored in kindness, understanding, and the courage to pursue dreams unceasingly.

But as he mulled over these dreams, Alex also felt the weight of responsibility resting heavily on his shoulders—an emotional weight that illuminated hope and trepidation alike. The future was unpredictable, and all he could do was orchestrate moments anchored in love while ensuring that the lessons steeped in understanding and growth would serve as the guiding light during storms.

In this world filled with uncertainty, patience and adaptation would become as important as any lesson he hoped to impart. The meta-conversation of choices, he realized, would unfurl continuously as Alex would journey alongside Ethan.

As he held this thought, the image of his father crystallized yet again, and he remembered one particular lesson taught during a simple, quiet moment—the art of patience. "Building a garden takes time, son. Plants won't bloom overnight; they need light, nourishment, and care. Just like us, people grow, evolve, and flourish when given the right conditions."

His father's words echoed softly in his mind, revitalizing his resolve to nurture a sense of patience in Ethan as they embarked on this journey together. He envisioned teaching his son that it was perfectly acceptable to take things slow; growth came not from rushing towards a destination but embracing each step along the way.

As evening crept in and stars began to twinkle in the night sky, Alex felt a sense of clarity wash over him. He would not only be imparting lessons or ideals but instilling a spirit of resilience, curiosity, and love that, with time, would flourish into something beautiful.

In the distance, the laughter of children echoed through the streets, a harmonious symphony intertwining with his dreams. The world was vast, with countless paths forming before him and Ethan, yet in that moment, Alex was reassured that as long as they navigated it together, with love at the helm, they would carve out their own unique legacy—one choice, one lesson, one bond at a time.

The Journey Continues

As I sit in the quiet of the morning, sipping on my coffee, the sun peeking through the window, I am enveloped in a profound sense of gratitude. Today is just another day in the long, winding journey of fatherhood, but somehow, it feels different—like turning the final page of a book that has been lovingly written over time. This feeling reflects the understanding that the story of a father is never truly complete but evolves continuously through the experiences and choices we make.

Being a father is akin to standing at the edge of an ocean, waves crashing and receding, each one representing a unique moment in time. Some waves bring joy; others, heartbreak. There are strong tides that challenge our footing, and gentle ripples that remind us of the beauty in simplicity. In these moments of reflection, I can see how each choice made, each challenge faced, further deepens the bond I share with my son and the understanding of who I am becoming as a father.

The journey of fatherhood is one that dispels the myth of perfection. There is no perfect parent; there is only the determination to show up each day, to nurture, to guide, and to learn alongside our children. The reality is that every day brings a new opportunity for us to grow—individually as fathers and collectively in our relationships. There are days filled with laughter, where I witness my son's unrestrained joy, and there are challenging days that push my patience and resolve. Both kinds of days teach me invaluable lessons—each is integral to this intricate tapestry of parenting.

It wasn't long ago that I stood at my own crossroads, torn between the nurturing love of my father and the rigid discipline showcased by my best friend's father. Each haunting memory still echoes within me, a reminder of the conflicts that shaped my early notions of masculinity and fatherhood. But as I embrace my role, I recognize that these experiences do not define the kind of father I must be today. Instead, they offer an enriched understanding, a foundation upon which I can build a new legacy.

In recent moments, I have watched my son traverse the challenges of growing up—climbing trees, falling down, and getting back up again. His little heart is emblematic of resilience; each scrape and bruise a testament to his determination. As he navigates this world, I find myself reflecting on my journeys—the moments of victory and those that left me feeling lost. I remember the warmth of my father's embrace during times of struggle, the sense of security it provided, and it dawns on me that my son deserves the same sense of safety in his explorations. I want him to know that it's okay to fail, that failure is not the end but a stepping stone toward growth.

I have come to believe that love is the grocery store of fatherhood. It is the sustenance that nourishes our relationships and supports development, allowing dreams to flourish. But just like any balanced diet, it must be complemented with other ingredients: patience, understanding, and discipline. Each of these elements plays a role in shaping our children's lives. It is in this blend that I find the essence of my fathering philosophy—the amalgamation of nurturing affection and necessary boundaries.

Patience, I have found, is a virtue taught through both the soft-spoken encouragement of my father and the stern lessons learned alongside my friend. It is born out of love—the love that makes us wait for our children to grow. It teaches our children to witness life unfolding, to understand that some things cannot be rushed. Each moment is precious; each lesson is a building block for their future. I often chuckle at how easily I have been tempted to hasten things along, to push my son to achieve what I think he should, only to remember the value of allowing him to find his own way.

And within those lessons of patience come moments where guidance feels like a game of tightrope walking. Just as I have learned to let my son explore, I must also be vigilant to ensure he learns boundaries. In these moments, regret often stands at the periphery, reminding me of the times my duties as a father felt overwhelming. But I embrace it all—the chaos, the noise, the unpredictability—as an integral part of the beautiful chaos that is family life.

In the quiet breaths of the afternoons when the world feels heavy, I seek solace in routine. The bedtime stories, the shared laughs, the rituals of meal preparation—each time I engage, I am weaving more threads into the fabric of our shared experiences. The simple act of storytelling unfolds moral lessons and ignites our imaginations. I've noticed my son's eyes widen as we delve into worlds of adventure, of bravery mixed with moments of vulnerability, and I realize how these stories are reflections of our own lived journeys—our challenges, our victories, our shared humanity.

But there is something deeper—a longing to ensure my son recognizes that it is perfectly okay to express vulnerability, to embrace the chaos of emotions that come with coming of age. I wish for him to learn that we all stumble, fall, and rise again, and that in those moments of vulnerability, there is strength. In the act of learning, he will find his own voice and his own way of navigating the world with authenticity.

Reflecting on my own father's teachings, I now understand more profoundly what became of his gentle embrace. My father created a sanctuary for emotions—a safe space where he nurtured my abilities and encouraged my exploration without the incessant pressure of competition. In fostering that sanctuary, he gave me roots, a foundation upon which to grow. Today, I strive to extend that legacy to my son, to cultivate his emotional intelligence and, more importantly, to teach him that expressing feelings is not a sign of weakness but a beacon of strength.

As I continue to explore this intricate dance of fatherhood, I also recognize the importance of community. The playground has transformed from mere play into a landscape rich with lessons shared among fathers. The laughter and chaos of kids playing hide and seek hide a more profound narrative—stories exchanged among fathers, their journeys documented in broad strokes of lessons learned. In their responses, I find reflections of my own struggles, and it reassures me that I am not alone in this dance of hearts.

In those shared moments, the fears of judgment dissipate, revealing the underlying truth: every father carries a diverse set of experiences and stories. Through shared vulnerabilities, there forms a bridge that connects us all. Within this umbrella of connection, we find strength, courage, and the realization that each day brings with it a new opportunity—a chance for discovery in this unpredictable exploration of parenthood.

And as our children grow, I know that it is also essential for me to grow. My journey as a father embodies an amalgamation of nurturing love, understood boundaries, and the willingness to listen and adapt. Balancing nurturing and discipline is not merely a duty, but a journey, one that plants seeds for future growth—both for my son and for myself.

The beautiful chaos that is parenthood nudges us toward change. I embrace all its imperfections as a critical aspect of my learning experience. For if every day is a new opportunity, then every moment becomes an invitation—an invitation to become better, more aware, more present, and more loving. They say the only constant in life is change, and so I find comfort in the fact that my journey, much like that of my son, is not linear; it is an ever-evolving tapestry painted with memories and dreams.

As this chapter in the narrative of fatherhood draws to a close, I invite you, dear reader, to reflect on your own journey—your own values, beliefs, and aspirations. Allow yourself to think back to the moments that shaped you, both joyful and challenging. Remember how you grew through each experience, how those experiences crafted the parent you are today.

There is no perfect guidebook for fatherhood, nor is there a singular measure for success. The joy lies in finding your rhythm, in embracing what resonates with you, and ultimately, in allowing the journey itself to guide you. Each day presents a new chapter, and as we write our stories, we create meaningful connections that stand the test of time.

As the sun sets and the day gives way to night, remember the beauty that is wrapped in those moments shared with your children: the laughter echoing through the halls, the lessons learned from simple mistakes, the chaos of the everyday woven into a symphony of love. It is the little things, after all, that often lead to the most meaningful growth.

With each choice made, you, too, are participating in a grand narrative, lovingly crafting your legacy one decision at a time. As we embark on this journey—together yet uniquely—let us embrace every moment with an open heart, knowing that while we navigate the uncertainties, we are all bound by the same hope and aspiration to be the best fathers we can be.

The journey continues, and with it, so does our capacity for growth, love, and learning. The pages of our lives turn and the stories unfold, reminding us, poignantly, that in the magic of every day, there exists an opportunity—a chance to do better, to love deeper, and to nurture fiercely. So let us embrace this journey, for it is in the unfolding chapters that we find ourselves and each other. The journey of fatherhood is not merely a destination but a beautiful, ever-evolving adventure.

–

Cheers to You!

Wow, what a journey it has been! As we wrap up this adventure together, I want to take a moment to express my heartfelt gratitude to you for sticking with me through every twist, turn, and revelation. It's readers like you who make this whole process worthwhile, and I'm genuinely thankful for your time and attention.

This book was crafted with love, sweat, and a sprinkle of vulnerability, and knowing that you've shared this experience with me fills me with immense joy. Remember, every page you've turned has not just been ink on paper; it's a reflection of experiences, growth, and the raw beauty of life. I hope it has inspired you in some way or at the very least provided a chuckle or two!

As you close this book, I encourage you to carry these insights with you into the world. Let them simmer, ponder, and influence your thoughts and actions. You have the power to embrace change, tackle challenges, and continue your own storytelling. Remember, life doesn't stop here; it's a continuous journey full of new chapters and endless possibilities.

So, let's not view this as a goodbye but rather a 'see you later!' I can't wait to hear about your own adventures, challenges, and triumphs in this beautiful, chaotic world. Share your stories, resonate with others, and let's keep the conversation alive. There's so much more to discuss, and I'm excited for what the future holds!

Keep that spark within you ignited, and remember to dive into every experience you encounter with the same passion and curiosity that brought you here. Thank you for being a part of my journey, and until our paths cross again, stay wild and stay wonderful!

With endless gratitude and excitement

Oluremi Makinde

Made in the USA
Columbia, SC
10 May 2025

57577453R00115